Divorce Is a Mitzvah

Divorce Is a Mitzvah

A Practical Guide to Finding Wholeness and Holiness When Your Marriage Dies

Rabbi Perry Netter

Afterword by Rabbi Laura Geller
"Afterwards: New Jewish Divorce Rituals"

JEWISH LIGHTS Publishing
Woodstock, Vermont

Divorce Is a Mitzvah:
A Practical Guide to Finding Wholeness and Holiness When Your Marriage Dies

Grateful acknowledgment is extended to the following for permission to reproduce their material in this book:

"Foreword," from *What Every Woman Should Know About Divorce and Custody* by Gayle Smith and Sally Abrahms, copyright © 1998 by Gayle Smith and Sally Abrahms. Used by permission of Perigee Books, a division of Penguin Putnam Inc.

"Afterwards: New Jewish Divorce Rituals" by Rabbi Laura Geller was adapted from an article first published in *Reform Judaism* magazine, published by the Union of American Hebrew Congregations.

Library of Congress Cataloging-in-Publication Data
Netter, Perry.
Divorce is a mitzvah : finding wholeness and holiness when your marriage dies / by Perry Netter.
p. cm.
Includes bibliographical references.
ISBN 1-58023-172-1
1. Divorce. 2. Divorce—Religious aspects—Judaism. I. Title.
HQ814 .N47 2002
306.89—dc21 2002006656

10 9 8 7 6 5 4 3 2 1

Manufactured in the United States of America

Published by Jewish Lights Publishing
A Division of LongHill Partners, Inc.
Sunset Farm Offices, Route 4, P.O. Box 237
Woodstock, VT 05091
Tel: (802) 457-4000 Fax: (802) 457-4004
www.jewishlights.com

DEDICATION

To
Elisheva Miriam,
Moshe Tzvi,
and
Shira Aviva:
The pupils of my eyes,
The lights of my soul,
The blessings of my life,
For whom I thank God daily.

CONTENTS

ACKNOWLEDGMENTS

I have lived with the writing of this book for over two years, which, I am told by those who know better than I, is not a particularly long time in the life span of a large writing project. Yet, for someone as naturally impatient as I, the task of writing this book has at times seemed daunting and endless. More times than I care to admit, I have wanted to abandon the project in favor of something more immediately tangible. That I didn't is a testimony to the encouragement of many people whose love and support I want to acknowledge publicly.

My family has been a wonderful source of strength and inspiration to me through this journey. My children—about whom I never tire of talking, of whom I am indecently proud—have made the greatest sacrifices that allowed me to write this book. I am enormously thankful that periodically they graciously gave up the part of my time that really belonged to them. I trust they will forgive me for the times their needs went ignored, and I pray that nothing in this book will embarrass them.

The first eyes to see everything in this book, and without whom there simply would be no book, belong to my friend, my confidante, my assistant, Cori Drasin. Cori lovingly and devotedly read every word and reacted with gentle criticism and unbounded support. She spent hours putting the manuscript in order—a task beyond mere mortals.

I am blessed to have a cadre of gifted and talented friends who belong to my community and who graciously read drafts of the manuscript. David Lauter is a thoughtful editor, who helped crystallize my thinking from the beginning of this project and helped save me from serious blunders. Rabbis David Ellenson and Michael Berenbaum were important voices for tradition and authenticity and were my teachers in conceptualizing this book. Julie Barroukh gave me invaluable direction, and Spencer Krull is responsible for much that is good in this book. I am deeply indebted to Adryenn Cantor for helping me think about the issues regarding mediation and litigation. Her candor, expertise and openness were invaluable in the preparation of that chapter. As always, the responsibility for any mistakes or errors lies solely with me.

My editor, Donna Zerner, has been a gift. I am deeply awed by her wisdom, her insights, and her talent as a very close reader. The readers of this book owe her a debt of gratitude that they are unaware of. Her unbounded devotion to this project has been a blessing and has surpassed any professional obligation. The many dedicated people at Jewish Lights Publishing have been an inspiration to work with, in particular Emily Wichland and Bridgett Taylor. The vision of Stuart M. Matlins, publisher of Jewish Lights, is what makes Jewish Lights the premier Jewish publishing house in the English language, and it is a consummate privilege to be associated with him and his stable of authors.

I especially want to thank the good people of Temple Beth Am in Los Angeles for entrusting me with the sabbatical time I needed to begin this book. I hope and I pray that the final product is a source of pride for them and makes the time they lived without me ultimately worthwhile.

Finally, I want to express my profound gratitude to the many men and women who shared their personal stories with me, who trusted me with their pain, their anger, and their fears as well as their joys and their triumphs as they made the transition through the stages of divorce. I have learned much from them, and I hope I have sufficiently camouflaged their identities so that they are the only ones who will recognize their stories contained here. May those stories help others to grow through, and heal from, their divorce.

Introduction

The voice on the other end of the phone sounded tired, sullen, and heavy with sadness and grief. "Rabbi," he said, his voice barely audible, "I have been married for eleven years. I have three children, ages four to nine. And last month I moved out of the house. I need to talk to you."

David had grown up in a typical middle-class American home. He and his brother were the sons of a businessman father and a social worker mother. He went to college and graduate school, pursued a career, married his college sweetheart, fathered three healthy and loving children, and even bought the proverbial home with the white picket fence. All the elements for a successful life were firmly in place.

And now his life was in turmoil, and he was living through chaos. The fabric of his world was unraveling, and he was the one pulling the threads.

What did he want from me?

What was David looking for in the office of his rabbi? Was he unilaterally terminating his marriage, coming to this rabbi/priest in search of absolution? Was he coming because he wanted to be told that his religious tradition holds that what he was doing was wrong? Was he coming because he needed therapy, and a rabbi gives free sessions? Was he coming because he felt alone, abandoned by God, afraid of being shunned by his community, needing reassurance?

What did he want from me?

David entered my office dressed in old jeans and a gray sweatshirt. An unusually articulate and talkative man, David had difficulty making eye contact. He slouched in his chair as we spoke, his shoulders hunched over, his chin almost touching his chest, his voice soft and sad. He spoke at some length about the anguish of living in a loveless marriage. He spoke of the years he had lived without emotional and physical intimacy with his wife. He spoke of his radical disappointment, of the sadness of losing everything he had worked for, of the ache of living without his children, of the despair that had come with feeling that he was going to have to start over. He could not shake the feeling that he was a failure—as a husband, as a father, as an adult. He was able to succeed in all other aspects of his life; why couldn't he make his marriage work?

He wondered: Was he inflicting irreparable damage upon his children? Were they going to be crippled emotionally from this rupture in their family life, unable to adjust to these changes in family structure, unable to trust authority figures because their parents had cracked the foundation of their world? Would they be capable of forming healthy, rewarding, stable, loving adult relationships when they grew up?

The guilt he felt was enormous. How could he look God in the eye? Was God disappointed with him? Was God angry? Was God judging him as a sinner?

So many questions. These are the questions I grapple with in this book.

And then David asked the question that had brought him to me, to his rabbi: What did Judaism have to tell him about this moment in his life? What guidance, what strength, what insight could he derive from his religious tradition? How could he make sense of his life at this juncture in a way that would be consonant with religious truths? If religion had nothing to say to him at this crisis in his life, then religion had nothing to say to him. Period. I was his rabbi; I was supposed to have the answers.

What he didn't know—what he couldn't possibly know—was that I was going through a similar experience. By the time he and I met, Esther and I had already made the decision to end our marriage; we would not go public with the announcement for another few months. I also had been struggling for some time to make sense of an unfulfilled marriage, of living with the pain of disappointment and loneliness, of trying to understand how and why the decision to end a marriage is made, of wrestling with the consequences of divorce.

So many questions.

As a rabbi, I am consumed with answers. My role—as presumptuous and as pretentious and as impossible as it is—is to have every conceivable answer on the tip of my tongue, just waiting for its question to be asked. David came to my office because he expected answers from me. But what he got from me instead was as unsettling as it was frustrating.

I took from my shelf a traditional collection of medieval Jewish commentaries on the Bible. I opened the book and began reading to David the beginning of Chapter 24 in the Book of Deuteronomy, which contains the biblical statement on divorce:

> A man takes a wife and possesses her. She fails to please him because he finds something obnoxious about her, and he writes her a bill of divorcement, hands it to her, sends her away from his house (Deuteronomy 24:1). [All biblical translations follow the text of the Jewish Publication Society Torah Commentary.]

Contrary to the contemporary stereotype, divorce is not a malady of modernity. Divorce has been around as long as there has been marriage. There it was, in black and white—as much a part of the biblical tradition as the giving of the Ten Commandments and the splitting of the Sea of Reeds.

I pointed out to David that on the same page as the biblical text are collected the commentaries of the preeminent medieval Rabbis. To the uninitiated, the names are strange, distant, foreign.

But individually and collectively, these medieval scholars provide the normative reading of the biblical text within Jewish tradition. I moved my finger along the page, pointing out to David the writings of one commentator after another. We searched, but we found not a word of commentary on divorce. On the question of the meaning of divorce, on the question of the propriety of divorce, on the question of approval or disapproval of divorce, there was not a hint of opinion. There was, as we were to discover over and over again, silence. Articulate, thorough, thoughtful medieval sages were uncharacteristically mute.

Only the preeminent biblical commentator Rabbi Shlomo Yitzhaki, who lived in the eleventh century in Troyes, France, and is best known by his acronym, Rashi, had something to say. His words are stunning, shocking, startling. On the biblical command to write out a bill of divorcement, he said, quite simply "Divorce is a mitzvah."

The words are almost scandalous. A mitzvah is commonly understood to be a good deed, something every Jew should aspire toward, an act full of holiness that fills the world with the presence of God. A mitzvah is something we are supposed to do.

What did Rashi mean, that divorce is a mitzvah? Was he advocating the termination of marriages in the same way he would advocate keeping the Sabbath, or the dietary laws, or honesty in business, or the giving of charity?

The answer, I believe, is both yes and no. A mitzvah is not merely a good deed. A mitzvah is a response to the voice of God commanding us to behave in a particular way. A mitzvah is an obligation. It is this understanding of divorce, I believe, that we can learn from Rashi. A divorce is not to be pursued, of course, but should a separation between husband and wife be warranted, obligations are imposed on the spouses that contain all of the weight of God's commanding voice.

This, then, is what I believe Rashi was teaching us: Just as marriage is initiated with certain and specific obligations in Jewish tradition, just as marriage is entered into with ritual acts and a legal document, known as a *ketubbah*, so too is marriage terminated with ritual acts and a legal document, known as a *get.* Marriage and divorce could not be more different in the way they are experienced, but Rashi teaches us that the painful in life has no less a requirement to be experienced with holiness than does the joyous. To seek the holy and the sacred is what I believe to be the central question governing divorce, as it is the ultimate question of every aspect of personal life: What are my obligations as an individual, as a spouse, as a parent, as a child? What does God expect of me as I struggle with the seemingly infinite decisions that surround divorce? How can I go through this crisis without destroying my soul in the process?

If the silence of the medievals is troubling, even more baffling is the silence of our contemporaries, at a time when divorce is abundantly prevalent.

"Of the making of books there is no end," said the ancient author of the biblical Book of Ecclesiastes. Indeed, in a recent catalogue of Jewish books from a company boasting the largest inventory of the latest publications of Jewish interest, there is a wide selection of very good and useful books on the human lifecycle. The life-cycle section lists five books on birth and baby naming, eight books on Bar/Bat Mitzvah, and six books on dating and marriage. One can even find five books on *taharat hamishpachah,* the laws of family purity, or the ritual use of *mikveh* in regulating a couple's sex life. There does not seem to be a lack of sources to guide people through the stages of life. But not a single Jewish book on divorce was offered. Again—still—the Jewish community is silent.

Jewish religious leaders and thinkers do not have a monopoly on silence. In a mailing from a major distributor of Christian books, I found an offering of thirty titles of resources on marriage. The hidden agenda for the proprietors of this book catalogue, of course, is the strengthening of marriage to avoid the pitfalls that lead to divorce. But not one book was listed that offered guidance on the subject of divorce. Not one.

It is not as if no one had ever written on the topic of divorce from a Jewish perspective. As we will see, attempts have been made.

But for a multiplicity of reasons that we will examine, the results have not been helpful. I found no book that I could put into the hands of the many family members who found their way to my office—women and men in pain and confusion and chaos because they were going through divorce—that would serve as a comfort, as a guide, as an inspiration, as a source of strength.

If earlier generations of religious leaders were silent, we can offer excuses. They did not confront a large incidence of divorce. They were easily distracted by other issues that were more pressing in their times and in their communities. They did not have enough experience with divorce to fully understand its dynamics. Or they simply did not know what to say. But we, who live at the beginning of the twenty-first century, can no longer afford the luxury of silence. Divorce is as much a part of our world as is the microprocessor and the cell phone, and almost as ubiquitous. If religion has anything to teach us about the fundamental values of life, divorce must be dealt with in an open, honest, and nonjudgmental inquiry.

This is what David was saying to me and what he was asking me for: to help him make sense of his divorce from a religious perspective. What wisdom did his Tradition offer him to shepherd him through this most difficult experience? What strength could he derive from the teachings of classical texts? What comforting words could restore his hope? What values could inform the difficult decisions lying in store from him? What questions should he be asking?

In a sense, I have been living with this book for years, both in my professional capacity as a rabbi and as a husband and father living through the experience of divorce. Like all clergy, I have seen families hemorrhage as husbands and wives go to war, where every decision is about winning and losing, where the only rule of the game is that the winner is the one who inflicts the most pain. I have sat with mothers who insisted that their ex-husbands could not stand on the *bimah* with their Bar Mitzvah sons because "he hasn't been a father to him all these years; he's not going to stand there as his father now." I have seen parents refuse to walk their daughter down the aisle together on the day of her wedding. I have seen fathers hide their financial assets and cause their children to live in poverty. I have seen enormous pain and suffering as a result of divorce. So much pain. And so much of it avoidable.

Psychologically, the effects of divorce parallel the trauma of losing a loved one. Divorce is a little death—or, more accurately, a series of little deaths. There is much to be learned from the wisdom of Judaism that helps us deal with loss and separation in general, and divorce in particular. At a time of radical transition, of alienation, of spiritual brokenness, wholeness can be found within Judaism. As painful as divorce is, not all the pain of divorce is necessary. Much of the trauma—for both spouses, for the children—can be minimized or avoided altogether. What I have learned from the many families with whom I have worked, from the authors and researchers whose words I have consulted, and from what I have been taught by my ex-wife and my children, who are my greatest teachers, fills this book.

The first lesson that I learned, one learned by everyone who ever contemplates divorce, is that divorce is one of the most difficult decisions any of us ever makes. Deciding to end a marriage is like deciding to amputate a limb. You know there is enormous pain in store for you. You know there will be a long period of recovery. You know you will be changed forever, in ways that cannot be anticipated. One thing is sure: divorce is not, as so many people think, easy. Not ever.

You know why there is so much divorce today? Because divorce is so easy.

I cannot count how many times I have heard this as an explanation for the sharp rise in divorce. You've heard it too—at dinner parties, in the carpool pickup line, standing around the soccer field, on talk radio. This truism can be heard anywhere, at any time. It is said with sufficient authority as to be believable simply on the strength of the conviction of the speaker.

It is no coincidence that the ones who believe this are either married or single, because no one who goes through it would ever say that divorce is easy. There is no one who was ever divorced who woke up one morning and said, "You know what? It's a beautiful day. I think I'll get divorced."

The decision to divorce is not arrived at cavalierly, capriciously, or on a whim—even if it might appear that way to outsiders.

My guess is that the notion of the ease of divorce comes from two places: the legal system itself, and the prejudice and judgment of married people.

Before the establishment of the no-fault divorce in 1970, a couple petitioning the court for legal dissolution of their marriage had to establish grounds for divorce, such as desertion, cruelty, infidelity, or other marital horrors. Whereas couples once had to demonstrate cause and to affix blame for the termination of their marriage, now divorce has been left to the discretion of the couple. It is true that it is easier to get divorced under a legal system that allows for no-fault divorce. It is also true that one can even be divorced without lawyers; Staples sells a divorce legal form kit for about $30, which will guide one to a divorce that will only cost the filing fees—about $300.

But to suggest that the simplification of the divorce procedure in any way mirrors the inner lives of the couple is to misunderstand the very nature of divorce. There is, of course, absolutely no causality between the easing of the restrictions governing the legal dissolution of marriage and the increase in the divorce rate. People do not dissolve their marriages because a divorce is on sale. Marital relationships are not terminated, family cohesion is not shattered, just because it is possible to get a deal.

The second source of the idea that divorce is easy is those married people who have endured difficult times in their marriages—that is, *every* married person. What married person has not harbored thoughts at one time or another of leaving? Most married people have experienced periods when the emotional cost of the marriage far outweighed the benefits, and they were ready to walk away, to seek refuge in solitude, to escape the pain and suffering of a difficult relationship. But most do not act on the impulse; they choose instead to persevere through the period of misery until they have worked through it. For whatever reason, they didn't walk out, and they remained in the marriage. For this, they deserve praise and admiration.

What they don't deserve is the right to judge others about their decision to separate. The internal dialogue that leads to the judgment is obvious. They figure, "If I was able to endure what I went through, they should have been able to. It can only be that people who get divorced are just weak and self-indulgent and narcissistic and selfish and lazy. They took the easy way out."

This became clear to me when I called a couple who were good friends of mine with the news that Esther and I were separating. I made sure both were on the phone so that they would hear it directly from me at the same time. His first reaction was to say to his wife—even before speaking to me—"Well, you see? It didn't happen to us." And then he proceeded to tell me of the effectiveness of their couples counseling, about all the good work they did in therapy, about how grateful he was that his marriage had endured.

His underlying message was that I should have worked harder in therapy. He was telling me that I had bailed on my marriage too soon. He was telling me that I was not the only one who had experienced marital difficulties, that if only I had his stamina and his character, my problems could have been worked through. He was telling me I was taking the easy way out.

But divorce is never the easy way out.

This statement, that divorce is easy, can be made only by someone who has never been divorced. It is an idea held by someone on the outside looking in, by someone who doesn't know the inner life of the participants, by someone who is clueless about what is in the souls of this man and this woman. I listen to someone say those words, that divorce is easy, and I suspect I am listening to someone who has harbored fantasies of being divorced—of once again being single, free from marital strife, liberated from familial responsibility, dating everyone in sight, feeling virile and vital—and presumes that this is the reason for the divorce. Those of us who have been divorced cringe at the sound of those words. Part of the reason for this book is the need to share with all who will listen some reasons for divorce that are reasonable.

We wish there were a formula that guaranteed the long-term success of marriage, but we recognize this wish to be magical thinking. We wish there were an immunity to divorce. We wish we could be given an inoculation to prevent divorce, but divorce is not an illness. It is a risk of marriage, a risk everyone takes who decides to marry. Even rabbis.

Esther and I met at a Jewish educational summer camp where we were both on the staff. She was twenty-one. I was twenty-four. We were young, full of energy and the idealism and the hopes and the promise of emerging adulthood. We shared core values and life goals: our vision of family, our work in the Jewish community, our religious beliefs and practices. All the fundamental ingredients for a fulfilling marriage were present. And she was the funniest person I knew.

I watched from a distance one day as Esther led a group of eight-year-old children in the game of "sticks." A simple, childish game. The kids played with intensity and joy, and Esther was completely present in the moment, making sure each child's needs were met. As I watched I said to myself, "This could be the mother of my children."

We have three: Elisheva, Moshe, and Shira. They are, as all parents will attest about their own children, bright and loving and caring and selfish and giving and happy and funny and fun and exacerbating and enervating—in short, an empire of contradictions, a constant source of wonder and amazement and *nachas*. They are the best part of life. They are the reason, I am convinced, that Esther and I married. For them, and because of them, I would do everything all over again.

I cannot imagine a couple more suited for each other than we were at the time we married. Seventeen years later we separated, dividing our home and everything in it. Our early dreams of building a home together were slowly transformed into the nightmare of negotiating a division of property. Everything we had built was reduced to just so much accounting.

How did this happen? This question has been asked of me, and by me, more than once. How did this happen: that a marriage that began with so much promise could end in divorce? What happened to us in those interior years between the poles of marriage and divorce—to us as individuals, to us as a couple, to us as a family? What changed, and why?

And other questions plagued me at the core of my soul. I am, after all, a rabbi, and the rabbi is supposed to be immune from marital problems. The rabbi is supposed to serve as the exemplar of the ideal Jewish family—at the very least, in the mindset of the members of my community, if not in my own mind. Would my divorce represent the ultimate failure of my rabbinate? Would I be ineffective as a religious leader if I was divorced? Would I be inflicting pain on the members of my congregation who harbored certain expectations of their rabbi, and who now would be feeling vulnerable in their own marriages? And what would it mean for me, for my family, for my career, if the answers to those questions were "yes?"

Those were my personal questions: questions that haunted me in the dark recesses of my soul, questions that I alone could ask of myself, questions that I alone had to answer. Each of us facing divorce has a series of unique questions. So many questions surround the experience of divorce, some particular to each divorced person, some universal and common to everyone. The questions David raised are questions faced by each of us going through divorce. Because I did not have satisfying answers to help David with his questions I was inspired to write this book.

This book is for the seemingly countless numbers of married people contemplating divorce who, like me, like David, struggle with the proper questions. Each chapter of this book responds to the most common questions surrounding divorce. My hope, my prayer, is that this attempt will begin to provide some answers as well. I offer this book to David, and to all the other Davids in the world both male and female, as a modest attempt to fill the gap, to end the silence in the Jewish world about divorce, and in a small way help to alleviate much of the unnecessary suffering and pain that seem to be so much a part of contemporary divorce.

1

THE EXISTENTIAL QUESTION: WHY IS THIS HAPPENING TO ME?

You are reading this book, I would imagine, because you, like David, are in crisis. Never in your darkest fantasies did you imagine that you would be in this position. The threat of marital dissolution is something that happens to other people. You know people who have gone through marital difficulties, who have separated and divorced, yet you never believed when you got married that it could happen to you.

Years ago, when you stood in front of your rabbi, in front of your family and friends, in front of the State, in front of God, you were filled with ecstatic hope for your future. The American dream was unfolding for you as you began your life with the one you were certain was your soul mate. You had experienced the magic of that moment of meeting, of the first kiss, of building an exclusive relationship, of dreaming of a life together. You probably endured the stresses and strains of planning the wedding, with its myriad decisions about location and invitations and guest lists and dresses and florists and photographers and caterers and seating and thank-you notes. You did all this because you were sure this was forever, and the wedding was the ritual of forever.

And now you have learned that forever is not a very long time.

What began as a fantasy full of promise, of hope, of possibility, of potential has now crashed and burned on the jagged landscape of a harsh reality. Relationships are enormously fragile, and marriage is among the most difficult of human undertakings. And now your marriage is falling apart, or has already come apart at the seams. You sowed in joyous song, but you are reaping in tears.

You agonize over the question: How did this ever happen to me?

You know you are a good person. Deep down you are kind, giving, loving, generous, compassionate, affectionate. You know you are capable of a relationship, yet you feel that this most important romantic relationship in your life is failing or has already failed. Inside of you is a battlefield of conflicting emotions: rage, fear, hurt, confusion, humiliation, disappointment, despair, embarrassment, shock, disbelief, denial.

And you are not alone.

There were 1,135,000 divorces filed in the United States in 1998, roughly one half the number of marriages in that same calendar year. Over 2 million adults and millions of children were directly affected by the turmoil of divorce. Millions of people in this country go through this experience each and every year. Barely a household in America has been untouched, in one way or another, at one time or another, by divorce. So much pain, so much anguish, so much instability.

How do we make sense of divorce? Why does there appear to be so much of it? What is it about society that seems to contribute to divorce, perhaps even encourages it? What has changed in family structures and in societal norms that makes divorce more prevalent today than forty or fifty years ago? If we can understand what takes place in the inner life as well as the outer life of one going through divorce, we may be able to go through the transition of divorce in a way that can bring us healing and wholeness, and not leave our souls injured by the process of terminating a marriage.

The answers to the above questions are by no means simple, and the attempt to reduce a complex matrix of the causes of divorce to a few easy answers risks the appearance of superficiality and simplicity. But the attempt must be made, nevertheless, because the question haunts. The question is asked, and it cannot be ignored. In fact, you are asking it now.

Why Am I in Crisis?

This is the question I asked over and over as I tried to make sense of my own experience. Time and again, over a very long period—as denial gave way to disbelief, only to be overpowered by denial once again—in fleeting moments of honesty and lucidity, I would ask, "Why is this happening to me?" Surely I should have been able to find the formula to fix my marriage. Surely there was a button to push, a technique to follow, a magical phrase to say that would restore the equilibrium of my marriage. I needed to understand what I was going through—and clearly I didn't.

This, then, is the place of beginning, the place where we must all start to make sense of our experience. The first mitzvah of divorce is to try to understand it—its psychology, its sociology, its ontology. The first mitzvah is to try to understand why this is happening at all. For there is no growth without understanding, no insight without knowledge, no healing without wisdom.

So I began to explore the issue through the world of words, both secular and sacred, to find meaning and clarity to guide me through this crisis. I was looking for information, insight, and wisdom from those who had walked before me in this garden. I began to read the studies of psychologists and sociologists who had devoted their professional and academic careers to understanding the duality of marriage and divorce. I searched the Bible and the Talmud, reading those ancient words in a new way, and from a new perspective, asking different questions of the text and deriving, for me, new understandings of the rich narratives. I discovered in those words a world of wisdom and compassion that shepherded me through the experience and helped me to grow through it.

The more I read, the more I discovered that there were good reasons why I was in crisis.

While it is true that every marriage is unique and distinct—governed, as it were, by the needs and wants and motivations and behavior patterns of the individual personalities of the husband and wife—it is also true that there are issues that affect every married couple. The intensity with which a marriage is affected by these issues can vary from home to home, and from marriage to marriage, but there is a commonality of experience that married people share. Marriages do not exist in a vacuum, unaffected by culture, history, and the values of the society in which we live. Relationships are shaped and influenced by a host of factors, some that are beyond our control and others over which we exercise complete mastery.

WHY IS DIVORCE SO COMMON?

I suggest four distinct yet interdependent phenomena that go a long way toward explaining the rise in the incidence of divorce in recent years. The first two are part of the makeup of human beings and have been around as long as there have been people; the second two are unique to our age. The categories I will explore are these:

- *The Psychological Factor.* Attraction to our mates is influenced by many factors, not least of which are subconscious impulses, desires, and expectations that are derived from early childhood experiences. Before we are married, we fantasize about what our marriages will look like. The reality rarely matches the fantasy.
- *The Developmental Factor.* Part of the process of human development—in fact, a defining characteristic in the stage of adult development—is to be in crisis during the transition from early adulthood to mature adulthood. The values, skills, and ideas that worked for us in childhood, adolescence, and early adulthood can no longer guide us along the adult life journey. Mature

adulthood means beginning anew. The choice of a life partner, a choice we often make in early adulthood, is reassessed and reevaluated as we emerge into mature adulthood. Sometimes we discover that decisions we made while young do not work for us as we age.

- *The Socioeconomic Factor.* Society has undergone radical changes in recent decades that have altered the structure of both the family and the marketplace, to the detriment of married life.
- *The Demographic Factor.* Personal life decisions, particularly in adulthood, are made differently today than in previous generations because of the simple fact that we are living longer. The blessing of longevity influences personal decisions—like whether or not to stay married—in ways that previous generations could not imagine.

Alone, each of these topics puts a strain on contemporary marriage. Taken together, these factors can make navigating in the waters of marriage extremely treacherous. Let's explore each of them in turn.

Why Were We Attracted to Our Mate?

Let us begin with the psychological factor. Our marital relationships are influenced by a constellation of forces. Some are beyond our control; others lie beneath our conscious minds. These forces are governed by a confluence of biology and psychology and sociology. Within every marriage, a subconscious drama hovers beneath the surface of every interaction and encounter between spouses. That drama is scripted by a combination of biological urges, universal psychological needs, and particular experiences from early childhood to emerging adulthood. Marriage attempts to fulfill our deep-seated psychological need for wholeness and security. This is its strength and also its tyranny.

Freud spoke of one of the goals of marriage—at the very least, for the man—as arising from a subconscious desire to replace the mother. He might not have been the first to suggest this. The Bible even hints at this idea in the story of the marriage of the second generation of patriarchs: the marriage of Isaac and Rebekah.

The background to the part of the story that interests me now is the arrangement of Isaac's marriage. Abraham, now old, advanced in years, facing his mortality, put his house in order. He had just finished burying Sarah, his wife of many years, the love of his youth. His attention turned to arranging a wife for his son, Isaac. This was the responsibility of the father in the ancient world.

Abraham did not want a local Canaanite woman for Isaac. He sent his servant, Eliezer, back to the ancestral birthplace, Aram Naharaim. There, at a certain well, Eliezer met Rebekah, the future wife of Isaac. When Eliezer saw Rebekah's beauty, her compassion, her kindness, her hospitality to strangers, he knew instantly that this was the woman for Isaac.

Jump forward a few biblical scenes. After arranging for Rebekah to come back to marry Isaac, the biblical story describes, in a few terse verses, the events of their meeting and their marriage.

> And Isaac went out walking in the field toward evening and, looking up, he saw camels approaching. Raising her eyes, Rebekah saw Isaac. She alighted from the camel and said to the servant, "Who is that man walking in the field toward us?" And the servant said, "That is my master." So she took her veil and covered herself. The servant told Isaac all the things that he had done. Isaac then brought her into the tent of his mother Sarah, and he took Rebekah as his wife. Isaac loved her, and thus found comfort after his mother's death (Genesis 24:63–67).

A remarkable narrative. The moment of meeting between Isaac and Rebekah is full of passion and romance. They see each other from a distance. Isaac is alone, walking in a field; Rebekah is on her camel. Their eyes lock, and, in the words of the talmudic Rabbis, Rebekah is "astounded" by Isaac. I would suggest an even stronger reading of the story: their eyes lock, and they fall madly, passionately, desperately in love. The Jewish Publication Society translation uses the word "alighted" to describe Rebekah's coming off her camel, but that is not what the Hebrew text says. In the original, the verb is *vatipol*, which means "and she fell off." Rebekah was so struck by the sight of Isaac that she fell off her camel.

That is passion. That is chemistry.

Isaac's act of bringing Rebekah into Sarah's tent as part of their marriage is startling, striking, even shocking. Why Sarah's tent? Why not his own? Why not a new tent? On one level, one can imagine reading this text with a Freudian perspective, namely, that Isaac was working out his Oedipal desire to sleep with his mother. But on another level, I think this narrative hints at another subconscious drama that plays itself out in every courtship and marriage, a drama which most of us are unaware of when we fall in love and get married.

Undoubtedly the most important decision of our adult lives is the choice of a life partner. Much of our waking energy, from the time of the onset of pubescence until we walk down that aisle at the wedding—and some of our sleeping energy as well—is devoted to preparing for marriage. We experiment with different people and different mating rituals until we find "the one." We struggle with desire and hope and expectations for a lasting relationship, only to be disappointed and hurt by the course of normal rejections and breakups. We move in and out of relationships until we find the person we believe is the one that God intended for us to spend our lives with.

But what are the things that first attract us to another? How do we understand chemistry—that elusive, yet critical initial attraction at the moment of meeting? What is it that makes us fall off our camels?

The answer is more complicated than one might imagine, for, as we stare deeply into the eyes of our beloved, powerful subconscious forces are unleashed. I think the biblical author understood this when it was written that Isaac brought Rebekah into Sarah's tent. The drama of all relationships, which plays itself out on the unconscious stage, is first written in infancy and continues to be written through each subsequent stage of development. It begins with the infant's attachment to mother, our first source of love and comfort and security and nurture. On a very deep level, we all hope to recreate those initial feelings of love and security when we fall in love. This is what Isaac was searching for, what Isaac needed, and what Rebekah provided for him: a subconscious reconnection to his lost mother, who, through her death, had abandoned him. Isaac saw instantly what Eliezer had also seen earlier at the well: Rebekah had many of the qualities of Sarah. That is why Isaac brought Rebekah into Sarah's tent; that is why Isaac was comforted. On a subconscious level, Isaac used Rebekah to replace Sarah.

Judith Viorst described this psychological dynamic in *Necessary Losses*:

> Our early lessons in love and our development history shape the expectations we bring into marriage. We are often aware of disappointed hopes. But we also bring into marriage the unconscious longings and the unfinished business of childhood, and prompted by the past, we make demands on our marriage, unaware that we do.
>
> For in married love we will seek to reclaim the loves of our early yearning, to find in the present beloved figures of yore: The unattainable parent of Oedipal passion. The unconditionally loving mother of childhood. And the symbiotic unit where self and other meld, as we once did before. In the arms of our own true love we strive to unite the aims and objects of past desire. And sometimes we hate our mate for failing to satisfy these ancient, impossible longings (p. 192).

What Viorst and others, like Lillian Rubin in *Intimate Strangers*, talk about is the idealized projection we all bring to our marriages. When we marry for the first time, we have no idea what marriage is like. We have seen marriages before. We grew up as part of the marriage of our parents, who were primary role models and who shaped many of our ideas about and expectations of marriage. Our parents provided for us our first experiences with love. They modeled how men treat women and how women treat men by the way they interacted with each other, with our siblings, with us. In a thousand subtle ways they defined for us gender roles and responsibilities.

Similarly, we know other married couples who had grown old together, others who had just begun their marriages, and still others whose marriages ended in divorce. But we never really knew marriage from the inside, the way it is lived day to day. The best we can do as we begin our marriages, therefore, is to project a fantasy about what married life will be like. We fantasize that married life will bring us stability. We expect that our marriages will be the bedrock upon which our entire reality is founded. This central relationship in life is given the task of providing reliability, constancy, interdependence, intimacy, nurturing, security, happiness. With and through the other we hope to achieve personal growth and spiritual fulfillment.

And then we learn that reality is never like the fantasy.

Somewhere along the way we discover that the one we married is an autonomous person, with his or her own history and baggage, with his or her own matrix of needs and expectations. We learn that our spouse is not our mother or father and that the love we need to achieve with our spouse is fundamentally different from the love we had in infancy. We learn that loneliness is not erased completely by marriage, that fulfillment is not provided solely by another person, that intimacy is fleeting and difficult to achieve.

This realization of the difference between fantasy and reality is the first crisis of marriage: a crisis every married person faces. It is a sobering moment that is necessary for adult growth and mature marital love. But it is also a moment—or series of moments—that, coupled with other factors, can destroy a marriage.

Growing Up, Growing Apart

Which brings us to the second factor affecting divorce: the developmental changes every adult must endure. Each and every human being emerging into adulthood, male and female, is required to navigate another internal landscape as well—a landscape that is uncertain, unsettling, unstable, and often terrifying. Fundamental to the process of maturation and aging is a series of physical and psychological stages that we pass through. Each of us, whether we like it or not, whether we want to or not, must eventually grow up, and that is a scary thought.

One of the most famous stories in the Bible is also one of the most troubling, perplexing, and painful. It tells of the first Jewish family. It is a narrative that speaks about family systems, about parent-child relationships, about growing up, about facing one's crucibles, triumphing over them, and emerging as a new adult. In Jewish tradition the story is known as *Akedat Yitzhak*, the story of the binding of Isaac. It is almost certainly the most discussed and commented upon biblical narrative, and it is the inspiration for much artistic activity. It is a story so compelling, so mysterious, so engaging that it pulls us back into it again and again.

It is a horrific story. God tests the patriarch Abraham by asking him to take Isaac—his son, his only son, his heir apparent, the future leader of the Jewish people—to an unknown place where he would tie Isaac to an altar, slaughter him, and offer him up like an animal as a sacrifice to God. This is the story of a God who asks the father of a people to kill his child.

This story makes my soul tremble.

The story is remarkably sparse in detail. Abraham arises early in the morning, saddles his donkeys, takes his servants and Isaac, and the wood, and the flintstone, and the knife. They travel in silence for three days until they come to the place. Abraham and Isaac go up to the top of a mountain, where Abraham builds an altar. He lays Isaac on the altar, binding his hands and his feet. Abraham then picks up the knife and raises his arm. Just before Abraham is to slaughter his son an angel calls out and stops him, telling Abraham to replace Isaac with a ram and to spare his son.

All's well that ends well, someone once said. At least, that is the way it appears on the surface. But underneath the story line of this biblical narrative lies a plethora of questions, a host of theological challenges, and many different possibilities to understand the story. I want to examine just one idea that flows from this narrative.

Most commentators identify Isaac as being twelve years old at the time of this incident, which would make Abraham appear to be an abusive father prepared to inflict the ultimate act on his son simply because he hears a divine command. In this reading, Abraham is the poster child for religious fanaticism. A fanatic is someone who believes what he believes so strongly that he is prepared to give up *your* life for it. So, against the child's will, the father's religious vision is imposed.

My favorite reading of this story is by the second-century sage Rabbi Yitzhak, who suggests that Isaac was thirty-seven years old at the time of the *Akedah* (*Breishit Rabbah* 56:8). In this version, a grown man willingly allows himself to be bound on the altar. How could Isaac allow himself to be placed on that altar? Not a word of protest? Not a struggle? Not an attempt to flee? Not even a muted cry for help?

My hunch is that Isaac went up on that altar because he understood this experience, in a metaphoric sense, to be the destiny of every adult. This was a watershed event in Isaac's life, a defining moment in his personal narrative. Because the painful reality is that there comes a time in every adult life when we have to go up on that altar and die to our past in order to inherit our future. There comes a time for us to let go of the person we used to be in order to embrace the person we are destined to be. This is the transition from one stage of adulthood to another.

Isaac goes up on that altar to symbolically die to his past, to leave his childhood. He has to leave his father in order for him to become the patriarch he is yet to be. That process, part of every human journey, feels to all of us like a crisis.

Most of us are aware of the stages of human development from infancy to childhood to adolescence. Each of these stages is very well charted and follows predictable patterns. Babies cut teeth within a few months of one another. Toddlers take their first steps at about the same time. We continue along this course, following the charts, until we come to adulthood and have "grown up."

William Bridges discusses this in *Transitions: Making Sense of Life's Changes.* Most of us think of adulthood as a level field between the teenage years and the golden years. We arrive at adulthood, and we function like machines, like automobiles. We function until something goes wrong, and then we open up the hood, replace the broken part, close the hood, and return to the road. Essentially, we view ourselves as if we were appliances.

I was commiserating with a member of my congregation while he and I were simultaneously recuperating from appendectomies. He observed, "You know, it's funny: when you're in your twenties, you sit around with your friends and talk about your china and your furniture. When you're in your thirties, you sit around and talk about your children. And when you're in your forties, you sit around with your friends and talk about your surgeries."

That minor surgery was the first time I felt the vulnerability of growing older and being susceptible to illness. And this comment, meant as a joke, clued me in to something so simple that I had missed it: I am not who I used to be. I am changing. My body is different; my soul is different. Sometimes life's most profound truths are the most obvious. We continue to grow, to change, to make transitions from one stage of life to another, even through adulthood.

The Swiss psychologist Jean Piaget is most noted for his contributions toward understanding the cognitive and emotional development of children, from infancy to adulthood. Piaget showed us that children are complex individuals who grow through distinct stages of development, each stage bringing new skills to be learned, new abilities that were not present before, new challenges to be mastered. With the work of Piaget, parenting changed, education changed, teaching changed, the world changed as we adopted his model of childhood development.

But Piaget was not the first to suggest that humans go through these transitional stages. As early as the second century there was a rabbi who established a paradigm for human development. His name was Judah ben Tema. These are his words as we know them:

> He used to say: At (age) five to Scripture, ten to Mishna, thirteen to religious duties, fifteen to Talmud, eighteen to wedding canopy, twenty for the chase, thirty to fullness of strength, forty to understanding, fifty to counsel, sixty to old age, seventy to ripe old age, eighty to remarkable strength, ninety to bowed back, and at a hundred he is like a corpse who has already passed and gone from this world (*Avot* 5:21).

Three of the first four entries are related to a curriculum of study within the classical rabbinic world. When a child is of the proper age, study of sacred texts should be introduced according to a hierarchy of difficulty and seriousness. Judah ben Tema understood that humans grow through stages, and learning must be age appropriate.

The remaining entries proceed by decades. We in the twenty-first century surely would not make the same choices in education and marriage that Judah ben Tema made in the second century, but I am struck by how remarkably intuitive the remaining ideas are. They are as applicable to our day as they were in the time of Judah ben Tema.

The division of the adult stages of development by decades is in some sense artificial. The changes we undergo as adults do not come as predictably as those of childhood. They do not take place within a window of a few months of each other. For some of us, the process begins in our early twenties; for others, it can begin in our late twenties or even our thirties. Nevertheless, the words of Judah ben Tema work as an apt metaphor of life's journey.

At the age of twenty, for the chase. This is the decade of the acquisition of skills, of position, of influence, of power, of wealth, of status, of love. Or at the very least, this is the decade for laying the foundations for the acquisition of these things. In our twenties we stand at the foot of the mountain of adulthood. When we are in our twenties, we make most of our major life decisions: where to go to school, the choice of a career or business, who will be our life partner, where we are going to live. Some people make these decisions early in the decade; some postpone them until later. Some marry and have children young, some postpone a family life in pursuit of a career; some do both at the same time. But at some time during this decade, these major life decisions are made.

At the age of thirty, to fullness of strength. It is no accident that it is in their thirties and forties when most people get divorced. Here is why.

When we are in our thirties, we live out our life choices as we climb the mountain. This is the time when strategies for advancement in career and business are established, when everything we have learned in preparation for a career is being implemented. This is the decade of achievement, when we prove we are capable of being who we intended to be. The thirties is the decade of honing skills, of gaining experience, of accruing wisdom. That only comes from making actual on the ground, day by day, what we had intended for our lives.

This paradigm holds true for marriage and for home life as well.

At the age of forty, to understanding. Understanding comes from knowing which questions to ask. The forties is the decade for spiritual depth, for a view of life from the middle of the adult mountain.

When we are in our late thirties to early forties, we evaluate our life choices. This is an age for being deeply reflective and philosophical. We ask the ultimate questions of life, in ways we tried but were unable to achieve in our youth because we didn't really know which questions to ask when we were young, because we didn't have enough life experience then to even begin to understand which questions to ask. We ask serious questions of meaning in our forties: Is my career fulfilling? Is this really what I want to do? Did I choose the right life partner? What does my life mean? Is this what I want out of life? How will I face my death? Is this all there is? What happens when this is over?

Serious questions. Painful questions. Terrifying questions.

Quite often, as people begin to answer these questions they discover that disappointment and angst have been constant companions. Many feel a crippling sense of failure. This is normal. This is part of the process of growing through adulthood, because the truth is that when we projected in our twenties what life was going to be like in our forties, we created, once again, a fantasy. That fantasy was all we had, because we lacked the experience to know any better how life works, or doesn't work. But, once again, reality is never like the fantasy. Inevitably, we find that what we fantasized our life would be like when we were in our twenties is much different from the reality of our forties. This is true even for people who achieve tremendous economic, social, and political success. And when that reality hits in all its fury, for most of us it feels like a crisis. Hence the popular term "midlife crisis."

I cannot count the many conversations I have had with people in my office, in hospital rooms, at parties, where I hear these stories. "Rabbi, when I went to law school, I thought I was going to make a difference in law. Now all I do is write letters. I want to do something else with my life." "Rabbi, I got into medicine because I wanted to heal people, not argue with accountants about how to practice medicine." "Rabbi, he's not the man I married; I don't recognize him anymore."

I hear these stories, as do all members of clergy, and I hear the pain and disappointment and confusion and fear in each voice. I have come to understand what these stories are about: they are about growing up. Because even adults continue to grow up.

Gail Sheehy wrote an enormously important book on the adult life cycle, called *Passages.* In it she writes,

> The work of adult life is not easy. As in childhood each step presents not only new tasks of development but requires a letting go of the techniques that worked before. With each passage some magic must be given up, some cherished illusion of safety and comfortably familiar sense of self must be cast off, to allow for the greater expansion of our own distinctiveness (p. 31).

In order to grow, to become the adult we were destined to be, we—like Isaac—must die to our past and be reborn to our future. This is fundamental to the adult life cycle. Sometimes, the love of our youth is the casualty of this process of development.

This is what it means when divorcing couples say they married too young. When they first made the life choice of a partner, the decision was based on who they were in their young adulthood. Often, as adults make the transition through the various stages of adulthood, the relationship that worked earlier in their lives has not developed along with them to accommodate who they have become. Mature love is able to change along with the people in the relationship; immature love dies on the vine. Mature love refuses to abandon the fight; immature love withdraws.

For a lump of coal to become a diamond, it must endure enormous amounts of heat and pressure. For romantic love to become the precious commodity of life, it must survive the crisis of midlife.

How Times Have Changed

All previous generations of marriages have faced challenges from the psychological and developmental factors discussed above. Yet, there used to be greater societal forces in play that provided a barrier against divorce. Primary among them was a sense of shame. Divorce was a *shonda*—an embarrassment for the couple and for their extended family, whose members often lived in close proximity. Cacophonous voices of family members surrounded the couple experiencing marital strife, enjoining them to reconcile differences, to make nice, to put aside personal grievances, to remain together if only not to bring shame on the family.

How times have changed. Divorce remains a source of sadness and grief, even shock, but the shame of it all has been lessened dramatically. Fewer people today remain married out of a sense of shame.

There are other socioeconomic factors that help us understand the age in which we live. Let us go back to the time when many of us were children and the world was a much simpler place.

Most baby boomers were weaned on a cultural diet of television shows like *Ozzie and Harriet, Leave It to Beaver, Father Knows Best,* and *Donna Reed.* Television at that time projected an image of the ideal family life in suburban America. Individually and collectively, these shows reflected a world full of order, predictability, stability, and harmony. They defined for us the prevailing notion of family life—or at least, the fantasy of what family life was supposed to look like. In particular, gender roles were absolutely clear and immutable.

Each day was relatively the same, following a predictable pattern, day after day, month after month. In the morning all members of the family would gather around the table for the first of the two family meals of the day. The husband and father of the house would go off to the office to engage in work that was always fulfilling and sufficiently lucrative. The wife and mother of the house, fully made up and dressed for the day, would wash the dishes that remained from the perfectly balanced and nutritional breakfast. The kids would be hustled out the front door to run to catch the school bus, which they never missed.

The family was clearly patriarchal, which is not to suggest that the matriarch's role was not important or that the wife and mother had no power. But the family functioned at its best when the man was the provider and the woman was the homemaker.

Home life was as ordered and structured in the evening as it was in the morning. Ward came home at night from the office to find June waiting with a kiss and a hot meal on the table. As the family sat around the dinner table, Ward solved Wally's adolescent problems, fixed whatever mischief the Beaver had gotten himself into during the day, and dispensed some folksy, fatherly wisdom at the end of the show.

The characters in these shows inhabited a world of calm and quiet; the problems of life were simple and naïve. Heroin chic was unheard of, as were gun violence, teenage pregnancy, gang-banging, and other pathologic states of modern life. Whatever problem was introduced in the beginning of the show would be resolved within the half hour, and at the end of every episode of *Ozzie and Harriet*, Ricky would sing.

The generation that created these shows wanted most of all to be married, have babies, own homes, mow the lawn on Saturday, attend PTA meetings, barbecue on Sunday, and take the kids to the ballpark. So they created suburbia, complete with its predictability and sameness. Jews bought into the fantasy of suburban normalcy as we moved out of urban centers into the suburbs. The veneer of stability provided by suburbia suggested that life was good.

And divorce was all but unknown.

And then came the sixties.

The Kennedy assassination. *The Feminine Mystique*. The Beatles. The Free Speech Movement. Vietnam. The birth control pill. Free love. It is not an accident that *Leave It to Beaver* went off the air in 1963. The world was changing. The baby boomers were coming of age. Sexual mores, family structures, society's norms were changing at lightning speed.

It is no wonder that the incidence of divorce in 1990 was double what it was in 1950.

According to the 2000 population census, the American families today that conform to the *Ozzie and Harriet* mold—mom, dad, 2.3 kids—constitute less than 25 percent of the total population. The structure of families in contemporary American society has become so diversified that social scientists have had to invent new categories simply to be able to talk about modern family life. We now have such categories as nuclear families, binuclear families, same-sex families, single-parent families, and blended families—categories that were unimaginable in the time depicted in *Ozzie and Harriet*.

We are living in an extraordinarily complicated and complex social environment, and the landscape is rapidly changing. One thing is abundantly clear: divorce is a fact of life, a phenomenon that in one way or another affects every household in America. If one's nuclear family is not affected by divorce, either by the parents getting a divorce or by one of the children getting a divorce, then someone in the extended family is likely to be divorced.

And remarried. Someone said that there used to be a time when parents had many children; now, children have many parents.

What has happened to cause so many changes in family structures? How is our world different from the world we inherited from our parents?

Women Come into Power

The single most profound difference, I would argue, is the enormous opportunity for personal growth and development for women as well as vast opportunities for economic independence as a consequence of the success of the women's movement. It is mind-boggling to ponder the differences between the choices available to my daughters and those available at the time my mother was coming of age. My mother had two options: to be Harriet Nelson or to be June Cleaver. My mother, like all women in her generation, was given the life script of being a wife and mother—a role that, fortunately, she played with relish.

By contrast, if the marriage pattern of my daughters is typical, they will marry at a later age than their own mother after they have finished graduate school and spent a few years pursuing their chosen careers. They will come to their marriages as mature women capable of sustaining themselves, not dependent on their respective husbands for economic sustenance.

How the world has changed for women. Roughly 2,300 years ago, the Rabbis created the *ketubbah,* the Jewish marriage contract, as a remedy to protect the woman in a world in which she had no economic power. In former years a girl grew up in her father's house. Her father, as the sole provider for her, had the power to decide where she was going to live, what she was going to eat, what she was going to wear, and whom she was going to marry. If the girl incurred any debt or caused any damage, her father was responsible to make financial restitution. He had the economic advantage, hence enormous power over her life. When she married, these financial responsibilities and obligations transferred to her husband.

The *ketubbah*, an enormously forward-looking and progressive legal advance—especially when we consider the age that produced it—is a lien against all current and future property of the husband as a corrective to his economic advantage and power over his wife. If the marriage was terminated by the premature death of the husband or through divorce, the woman would be given a sum of money sufficient to maintain a household for about a year. In this way, a woman and her children would not be abandoned, penniless, vulnerable. She would have the cushion of a year's income to allow her to put her life back together.

This is the way the world worked for hundreds of years, until our own generation, when women entered the workforce and achieved an enormous, albeit incomplete, economic advance.

Ironically, however, the entrance of women into the workforce, whether for economic or for ideological reasons, has been a major contributing factor to divorce. Many women in previous generations remained in unhappy marriages because they had no means of support other than their husbands. They had no choice but to stay. Having a separate career, having a job that provides an income separate from their husbands' income, has given freedom to a new generation of women. The lessening of women's dependence on men has enabled couples to separate who might not have divorced in another age and who probably should have.

A stunning statistic: Currently half of all divorces are initiated by women, one-third are initiated by mutual consent, and only one-sixth are initiated by men. Much has changed in the social fabric of American families as an unintended consequence of the success in lessening women's economic dependence on men. Foremost among the changes has been a transformation of marriage from a unit of economic production, which it had been for centuries, to a relationship founded on the romantic ideal of marriage as the source of emotional support, spiritual nurturance, and personal growth. The economic benefits of marriage are still important, but far less so with the increasing ability of women to earn income.

But with every blessing comes a curse. The blessing of women's rights and privileges brought the curse of the increased fragility of marriage as an institution. Marriage became more fragile, more vulnerable to dissolution, when the essence of marriage became the relationship itself. It is not surprising, therefore, that the rates of divorce began to rise in the 1960s.

And then came the eighties.

A Harder Road for Men

Just as modern life has changed the rules for women, it has changed for men as well. It is almost universally accepted that a man's most important role is to provide the primary income for the family. That has not changed, even with the advent of feminism. But the economic pressures on men have increased because the climate of the corporate culture has been altered. It used to be that a young man joined a firm and worked fourteen hours a day climbing the corporate ladder. By the time he reached his fifties, he was supposed to be in a position of senior advisor to the other young workers and spend much of his day in the country club or on the golf course, networking, bringing in business, and then turning over the job to some kid who was putting in fourteen hours a day. That was supposed to be the time when the company took advantage of his experience, took care of him, protected him, gave him security, and he planned for a comfortable retirement.

But the corporate world has changed, and the deal is over, and the climate is cruel and vicious. In the era of corporate downsizing, no one's job is protected. Everyone, no matter what age and experience, competes on a level playing field, where productivity is judged, not wisdom or experience. Where profits are rewarded, not loyalty. Where corporations have terminated workers of twenty-five years just days before their pensions were to kick in. Now, instead of relaxing in the clubhouse, men in their fifties are competing to keep their jobs with men and women two decades or more their junior. They still have to put in the fourteen-hour days, and there is no let up, and there is no taking it easy, because they know the company can replace them with younger men and women at two-thirds their salaries or replace them with a machine, or eliminate their position altogether. And they know the companies will do that to cut costs, to increase dividends, to remain competitive. More time is spent by men of this generation away from family life as a result of this change.

In spite of the enormous pressures and difficulties of contemporary family life, I would be the last to argue for a return to those days of gender-determined roles. It is cruel to women who want careers to insist that they cannot have them, and it is demeaning to deny women the same opportunities and choices as men; and it is dehumanizing to impose a life on someone because of accident of gender.

But families have paid an enormous price for the increased opportunities and choices available to women—opportunities that nevertheless should be embraced and celebrated. And families have paid an enormous price for the increased ruthlessness of the marketplace toward men. There is a cost to living life with this level of stress and time pressure.

Groceries still need to be bought, and dinner still needs to be cooked, and the kids still need to be schlepped to and from their appointments and lessons and activities, and the house still needs to be cleaned. The list goes on without an end in sight. The household burdens have not diminished because women have entered the workforce. Household chores are divided between family members, usually unevenly, and the consequence of dual-career families is that now everyone has more to do but less time and less energy in which to do it. The stresses and anxieties and tensions that come from this way of living are enormous, and for some they are toxic.

In many contemporary marriages, household chores are divided between the partners in ways unprecedented in earlier historical models of marriage. Spouses negotiate which tasks will be theirs—one generally does the cooking, while the other does the marketing, or the cleaning, or the scheduling of appointments—

based on personal proclivities and skills and talents. One may need to control the finances; the other may want nothing to do with finances. One may be great at household repairs; the other may cringe at the sight of a wrench. One may be great at cleaning the house; the other may not know how to use a broom. It doesn't matter which one does which task, as long as the chores are done and the household runs smoothly.

Except that it does matter. It matters a great deal.

It matters because, subconsciously if not consciously, the perception of marriage—and, in particular, gender roles in marriage—has not changed as rapidly as have our social institutions. Psychology has not kept up with sociology. While there are, obviously, exceptions, men still see their primary tasks in the family structure as being the principal providers. There is rarely a question about whether or not a man will have a career. In fact, men who stay home to care for children are considered an anomaly. It is the man's job to support the family. Women, on the other hand, still have primary responsibility in the home, even when they work outside the home.

A typical scenario, told to me over and over, by numbers of women:

A husband stops off at the grocery store to do the marketing after working twelve hours at his office. At work he fought his wars and won his battles, which, as we have said, are presumed to be his primary tasks. He has finished a stressful day of hunting game and thinks he deserves his quiet and his rest, his hot meal and his slippers, his newspaper and his pipe. But he has done the marketing, which he feels is above and beyond his responsibilities. After all, his father never went to the grocery store. Compared with earlier generations of husbands, he has evolved. When he comes into the house, he says, with not a little pride of accomplishment, "Honey, I'm home. I just went to the market. Isn't that good?"

The wife, on the other hand, began her day by getting the kids dressed, feeding five people breakfast, packing up three school lunches, choosing the right shade of pantyhose to match her business suit, throwing the kids into the car to drive carpool, and negotiating rush-hour traffic while trying to apply mascara and blush and breaking up a fight between the children in the back seat, all the while planning what she would say at the staff meeting on arrival at her office.

And it's not even 8:00 A.M.

That evening, when she hears her husband ask for recognition and approval for doing a single household task, she feels unappreciated, dismissed, and taken for granted, almost as if she had another child, not a partner. A button is pushed inside her, and she feels anger and resentment. Instead of being nurturing, she snaps at him: "What do you want, a medal?"

He feels hurt and unappreciated and rejected; she feels hurt and unappreciated and rejected. Often these feelings are not articulated, and they remain as festering resentments that have a deteriorating impact on their relationship—resentments that can build up over years.

This is not the life promised by *Ozzie and Harriet.*

HOW LONG CAN YOU STAND AN UNHAPPY MARRIAGE?

Finally, we must look at the fourth factor: the issue of demographics. One irony that results from the blessings of modern life—a factor that influences our evaluation of our life choices in our thirties and forties, is our increased longevity. When my grandfather died in 1963 at the age of sixty-five, he was not considered a young man. Most people who died in the sixties died in their sixties. If there had been bypass surgery in 1963, my grandfather most likely would have made it into his eighties. Today, bypass surgery is almost routine, and the average life span has been increased dramatically as a result of this and many other medical protocols.

Increased longevity helps explain the recent rise in divorce. In the generation of my grandparents, many couples remained married even though they were miserable, even though they often felt contempt for the other, even though there was no love. They remained married in part because of the calculation of the risk-benefit ratio.

The personal calculus affecting those evaluations of life choices is different when we look at twenty years of life ahead of us, like my grandparents, than if we look at forty or fifty years of life, like most people divorcing today.

If you are in your forties and looking at twenty years of life ahead of you, the decision to divorce makes sense only in an extreme case. Knowing that divorce creates psychic scars that take years from which to recover, and knowing that it may take years to meet the right person to marry, only to have a few good years together until one or both partners gets sick and needs care, makes one think that the pain one faces in divorce is too great a price to pay for the limited benefit of finding a more suitable partner. But if you are in your thirties or forties and looking at forty or fifty years of life ahead of you, the pain of living that long in an unhappy marriage can be greater than the pain of divorce. The possibility of spending many years in a second marriage that more closely approximates one's romantic ideal has a certain appeal.

And still, for some others, the thought of spending another forty or fifty years with this person is simply unbearable, regardless of whether or not they will find a more suitable mate. For some, even the prospect of living alone, as a single, is preferable to the marriage they are in.

Put these four phenomena together—the psychological, the developmental, the socioeconomic, and the demographic—and it becomes clear that not every marriage will make it. Not when marriage is founded on ideas of romantic love, not when economic interdependence does not keep two people together, not when social coercion does not shame people into staying, not when marriage is seen as an instrument of personal growth, not when our partners are required to be either our soulmates or nonmates.

Put these four phenomena together, and we can understand how the decision to divorce is the result of forces that are often greater than any single individual or couple. For the most part, divorce is arrived at not because of severe character flaws or because of the stubborn refusal of two spouses to make their marriage work. For the most part, divorce is the public recognition that this marriage is over, that this relationship has run its course, that you did the best you could, that you created a legacy that will serve you well as you begin the next chapter of your life.

2

The Hardest Question: To Leave or Not to Leave—How Do I Decide?

How does one decide to get divorced?

Some of you reading this have come to this book in search of an answer. After all, the rabbi is supposed to have the answer. And if you were to come into my office and ask me whether you should get divorced, my answer would be "I don't know." This is always my first answer, and always my last answer. The truth is, I don't know whether you should be divorced, and your therapist doesn't know whether you should be divorced. Not even your mother knows whether you should be divorced. There is only one person who knows, the one person who has to live with the consequences: you.

Divorce is an intensely personal decision. No two people experience divorce in exactly the same way, and what is good for one person may be disastrous for another. No couple going through divorce together experiences it in the same way. Divorce is a much different experience if you are the "leaver" or if you are the "leavee," if you are the one who has decided to end the marriage or if your spouse has left you. Moreover, what is right for you now may not be right for you later, and vice versa. There is no precise formula to follow, and there are no guarantees of a particular outcome. There are merely feelings to explore, issues to think about, truth to face, decisions to make.

The decision is yours.

Should I Stay for the Children?

One of the first questions of parents who are contemplating divorce, one of the first questions of grandparents and aunts and uncles and cousins and friends and even strangers, is, what would be the effects of divorce on the children? No decision about divorce can be made without thinking this question through.

There is a clear and unequivocal social bias that it is better for children to grow up in an intact family than to grow up in a divorced family. Without a doubt, growing up in a loving, nurturing, happy family with mama bear and papa bear and all the little baby bears sitting around the table is the familial ideal—a family environment containing the promise that children will grow up healthy, well-adjusted, grounded and centered, growing to be the best that they can be, capable of establishing and sustaining loving relationships in their lives. This type of family is also what we all thought we were establishing when we got married. But my guess is, if you had this idyllic scene in your home you wouldn't be reading this book.

Conflict and anger are normal in healthy marriages. It is impossible for people to live together without there being intermittent episodes of disagreement and anger. That children see their parents fighting is not necessarily psychologically damaging to them. On the contrary, for children to see their parents argue and then work out a resolution to their conflict is very healthy for them. An important life skill for parents to model is how to resolve disputes in a way that is respectful, dignified, equitable, and just. In a sense, arguing with each other allows parents to demonstrate the important art of compromise, without which long-term social relationships are impossible.

But we are not talking about healthy relationships now. We are talking about marriages in which there is unresolved anger, in which tension and conflict are a staple of the marital diet, in which affection and tenderness are essentially absent.

So the question really is, which is better for children: to grow up in an intact home with two parents, even though it is a home in which there is marital discord and emotional estrangement, or to grow up in homes in which their parents live separately? Or, to put it more concretely, will it cause greater psychological damage to your children if you get divorced than it will if you stay married?

The answer to that question is "yes and no." In other words, the answer to this question is enormously complex. The real answer is "it depends."

It is not true that children automatically fare better in intact families than in divorced families. There is considerable data to show that living with chronic marital distress has a deep impact on the emotional, psychological, physiological, and interpersonal development of children. Research has shown that the effects of marital conflict on children are profound. Children who grow up in two-parent homes in which there is chronic marital discord develop emotional and behavioral problems. These problems can find expression in external behaviors, like excessive aggression, vandalism, noncompliance, or delinquency, or in internal behaviors, like depression, anxiety, or social withdrawal. Growing up in a high-conflict environment can lead to a negative self-image and to distrust of a world that is perceived to be essentially hostile and untrustworthy.

In a family in which parents cannot handle their disagreements, in which anger and distress increase as time passes, in which conflicts are not resolved but prolonged, in which the marital relationship vacillates between rage on the battlefield, attack and counterattack, accusations and insults and emotional abuse on the one hand, and emotional apathy and disconnect and withdrawal and alienation on the other, the odds of raising healthy, well-adjusted children are slim.

The notion of remaining married for the sake of the children in this situation is ultimately hurtful and damaging to children.

Something has to change. This type of family dynamic screams for intervention. Serious therapy needs to be sought. Communication skills need to be developed. Intense spiritual work needs to be done. If you don't do this kind of work, if you don't invest the time and energy required to end marital discord, the negative impact of your marriage on your children will create remorse you will carry around with you all your life. If for no other reason, do this work for the sake of the children. But if, after a serious and honest attempt to fix the problems within your marriage, there remains discord because of a fundamental incompatibility between you and your spouse, divorce is a remedy that the Torah provides as a last resort to stop the combat.

SHOULD I STAY OR SHOULD I LEAVE?

Besides the issue of children, there are good reasons to be married, and there are other good reasons to be divorced. In fact, there are some very good reasons to be divorced. Here are three.

Abusive Behavior

Not every husband or every wife is expected to be loving and gentle and tender during every moment of marriage. Anger and rage erupt within every one of us, and even rabbis have been known to lose control of their emotions from time to time. But there is a line that can never be crossed: a line beyond which no excuse is acceptable, no attempt to understand is meaningful, and no rationalization is permitted. That line is domestic violence.

Domestic violence is defined as physical violence, threats, emotional abuse, harassment, or stalking to control the behavior of one's partner. Physical violence includes putting your hands on a person against his or her will, shoving, pushing, grabbing, pulling, or forcing someone to stay somewhere.

According to the American Bar Association Commission on Domestic Violence, recent studies show that between 25 percent and 30 percent of all women are abused—physically, verbally, or psychologically—by their intimate partner at some point in their relationship, while about 5 percent of men are abused by their intimate partners. At least one million women each year suffer nonfatal violence by an intimate, and roughly six thousand women are killed by their significant others each year. Rates of domestic violence remain consistent across racial and ethnic boundaries. In other words, Jews are not free of the scourge of domestic violence, although there is much shame and denial and too much silence on the subject of abuse in Jewish families.

These are frightening statistics. Chronic name-calling, shouting, physical assault, intimidation, threats, and terror are unacceptable behaviors under any conditions, and particularly within marriages. No one is required to live with someone who has a severe anger management problem. No one should live with the threat of danger.

An assault on another's person is more than a physical assault. It is an assault on the image of God that inheres in every human being. It is illegal, it is immoral, it is intolerable. It violates the dignity and sanctity of one created in the image of God.

As a rabbi I have three words of advice to anyone in a dangerously abusive relationship: Get out immediately. Do not pass Go. Do not collect $200. Even the threat of violence has no place in interpersonal relations.

I once asked a woman whose husband had beaten her up on several occasions why she stuck around after the first beating. She said, "You are never loved as much as you are right after an episode of beating. My husband would drop to his knees, wrap his arms around my legs, put his face in my lap, cry, apologize, beg for forgiveness, tell me how much he loved me, how much he needed me, how sorry he was, how ashamed he was, how it would never happen again."

But of course it did happen again. And again. She finally left, taking the kids with her.

It requires serious long-term therapy to help a chronic abuser change. It is a long, painful, arduous process to examine the subterranean psychological dynamics that lead to abusive behavior and to develop the mechanism to overcome them. But the first order of business is to remove the victims from harm's way and to ensure, as much as possible, the physical safety of family members. Separation, even divorce, is a must.

Finally, if abusive behavior toward a spouse is grounds for divorce, then even more so is physical, sexual, or psychological abuse of children a justified reason for divorce—if not jail.

Substance Abuse

According to the National Institute of Alcohol Abuse and Alcoholism, addictions to alcohol, prescription drugs, and illicit drugs have become prevalent in American families. Substance abuse is not bound by age, race, or social status. It affects millions of adults and children nationwide, including Jewish families. The effects of substance abuse on family life can be devastating, and addiction on the part of one spouse can be another very good reason to terminate a marriage.

One effect of addiction is an inability to meet work, school, or family responsibilities. When one spouse suffers from an addiction, the entire family is put at risk. What often happens in a family headed by an addict is that the dynamic of family life changes to accommodate the addiction. Spouses and children become complicit in enabling the addict to feed the addiction by covering up for the addict, making excuses, stepping in to fulfill the addict's responsibilities, denying the severity of the problem, and the like.

Intervention and recovery programs have been successful in assisting addicts to overcome their addiction and return to a functioning, productive life, and all efforts should be made to get the addicted parent into rehab. Support is available, and your rabbi will be able to assist in finding the right program. But in order for a twelve-step program or any other rehab program to work, the addict must make an internal decision to change his or her behavior. Short of that willingness, no threat or forced intervention or consequence will have any effect. Moving out of the house may be the only way to protect yourself and your children from the traumatic behavior of a substance abuser.

Infidelity

When I first came into the field as a rabbi, a man came to my office. He said, "Rabbi, I'm having an affair." I responded the way I thought I was supposed to respond, the way I thought someone thrust into a position of moral leadership was expected to respond, the way a religious authority was required to respond. I said, "What you are doing is wrong. You can't do that. You have to end it. Now." Isn't that what I should have said? The man looked at me, anger overtaking his demeanor, and said, "I know it's wrong. I don't need you to tell me it's wrong." "So why did you come here?" I sheepishly asked. "I came because I needed someone to talk to. I came because I need someone to help talk me through this. I came because I need to find someone who is supposed to have the wisdom to help me find my way out of this. But I see that someone is not you." And with that, he left my office. I never saw him again.

I was devastated. I had failed miserably in one of my first attempts at pastoral counseling. Instead of providing emotional and spiritual guidance at a time of great personal turmoil, I had assumed a moral posture that inflicted guilt, judgment, intolerance, and condemnation. It was as if I had brought the weight of thousands of years of sacred tradition to bear upon his head and spoke with no less authority than if it had been God's own voice. I spoke words that hurt.

It does not take a moral giant to know that infidelity is wrong. A clear text in the Torah forbids it, in a part of the Bible that everyone learns at a very early age. Infidelity is such a basic prohibition within society that it is part of the Ten Commandments. Just two words in the Hebrew: *Lo tin'af.* You shall not commit adultery. No historical narrative surrounds this Commandment to provide contextual meaning. No theological reason needs be given. No deep psychological discussion is provided. The truth of this prohibition is obvious—or should be. Just don't do it.

But if this man knew that what he did was wrong, why did he come to see me? First and foremost, I believe, he came because he needed to be heard and understood. He was alone with his guilt and his anguish. He needed to connect with another human being and unburden himself of his story. Second, he came because he was looking to hear another voice of God—one different from the judgmental one he already knew. Does God understand him and his motivations for what he did? Does God still love him, or does God hate him? Can God ever forgive him? Third, he needed to be reassured that he wasn't unique in this behavior. He needed to hear that he was not the only one who had made this mistake. And he wanted to explore why he did it, and how to stop it.

I wish I had another chance to talk with this man. I would tell him, initially, that I am sorry I was hurtful. I learned an important lesson from that experience: that no one has elected me an Israelite Prophet, hurling judgmental jeremiads of fire and brimstone. When someone comes into my office to talk, my first job is to listen. It is not my job to hear their words simply to prepare for a rabbinic response. I cannot do any good as a religious counselor if people coming in to see me don't know that my office is a safe place and that I am not rigid and tendentious and judgmental.

But I would also want to tell him that he raised a question that has remained with me all these years. The question is, why would people do things they know are wrong? It might seem like a simplistic, perhaps even naïve, question. But I believe it to be an enormously profound question, one we should take seriously. Why do people do things they know are wrong? What is the internal mechanism that causes conscience to be silenced, personal morality to be ignored, and resistance and restraint to break down?

One of this man's concerns was his desire to know that his behavior was not an aberration, even though it was morally indefensible. If I had the opportunity of meeting him again, I would want to read with him a narrative from the life of no less a figure than King David. It is a difficult story, told without literary fanfare, spartan in its detail. The story is told in the Second Book of Samuel:

> At the turn of the year, the season when kings go out [to battle], David sent Joab with his officers and all Israel with him, and they devastated Ammon and besieged Rabbah; David remained in Jerusalem. Late one afternoon, David rose from his couch and strolled on the roof of the royal palace; and from the roof he saw a woman bathing. The woman was very beautiful, and the king sent someone to make inquiries about the woman. He reported, "She is Bathsheba daughter of Eliam [and] wife of Uriah the Hittite." David sent messengers to fetch her; she came to him and he lay with her—she had just purified herself after her period—and she went back home. The woman conceived, and she sent word to David, "I am pregnant" (II Samuel 11:1–5).

The story is scandalous. David was the greatest of Israelite kings, beloved by his contemporaries, and adored by history. Tradition sees him as the author of the Psalms and the ancestor of the Messiah. God entered into a special covenant with David, promising that his descendants would occupy the throne of Israel in perpetuity.

Even one of the greatest leaders of Israel was guilty of severe moral infractions.

Why did David do it? Why did he have an affair with a married woman? At first blush, one might think the answer is obvious: because he could. He was a man and he was the king, and in the words of that great twentieth-century theologian Mel Brooks, "It's good to be the king." He saw a beautiful woman bathing. He wanted her. He sent for her. He slept with her. End of story.

But there is more to this story than the blush that covers it.

King David had multiple wives and hundreds of concubines. He certainly had no lack of sexual outlets. Surely there was someone in his retinue who could ignite his passion and fulfill his sexual needs. His desire for Bathsheba must have been more than mere sexual attraction.

I believe a hint is given in the opening verse of this narrative, which gives us the context of time. The story takes place "at the season when kings go out to battle," at the time of the year when kings would lead their armies on their campaigns of conquest. David was a warrior king, leading his troops over the years through one military victory after another, accustomed to being in the thick of battle. But this year, David sent his general to lead the troops in battle against the neighboring country of Ammon while he himself stayed home, holed up in his palace. David was aging: not yet an old man, yet too old to lead his troops in battle. Combat was an activity that remained for younger men. By the time of this episode, David had hit middle age and knew that his glory days as a warrior were over. That stage of his life, so much a part of his identity, was gone.

It is always difficult to analyze a patient who is not lying on the couch in front of you, but it seems rather apparent that King David was suffering from what has been called retirement neurosis. David was in crisis. His youth now behind him, David was confronting his mortality in a way that could not be eased by the bravery and courage that served him on the battlefield. Recognizing the inevitable, he looked into the face of the death that is brought about by time, over which we ultimately have no power. No longer a man's man, King David compensated for his loss of military prowess—and the loss of his youth—with a sexual conquest. He transferred his need for power and virility to a different battlefield.

Many people have suggested many different motivations for infidelity, and they are all essentially correct for some of the people, some of the time. But my experience has taught me that one unifying motivation for adultery underscores all the other reasons. At the heart of every extramarital affair—for both men and women—lies the fear of death.

The question nags at the depths of the soul: Is this all there is? Have I missed something? As one woman expressed it to me, "I cannot imagine that this is the last body I'm ever going to know." What

I hear in that lament is the fear that death will come, and life will have been incomplete, and experiences will have been missed, and lessons unlearned, and opportunities for growth and joy and love wasted.

The fear of death is an unforgiving and unrelenting master. It is with us constantly, buried deep in our subconscious and governing much of our behavior. Ernest Becker won a Pulitzer Prize for his book *The Denial of Death*, in which he talks about how much of what we do is directed by our need to overcome the finality of our deaths. That need to transcend our own nothingness leads either to positive and worthwhile activities or it leads to self-destructive behaviors. Adultery is one of those self-destructive behaviors.

There are serious consequences to adultery. The Torah understands infidelity to be an affront to God, who is the source of holiness. It is a violation of the covenant between husband and wife, a devastating betrayal that shatters the trust between the couple. It leads to feelings of rejection and humiliation and self-doubt. It decentralizes and devalues the marital relationship, which is never the same after the discovery of infidelity, even if the couple chooses to continue to live together.

Just two words in the Ten Commandments are required: *Lo tin'af.* You shall not commit adultery. No matter the reason, no matter the motivation, just don't do it.

Infidelity is one very good reason to get divorced.

But infidelity doesn't automatically have to lead to divorce, even though, admittedly, the Rabbis of the Talmud rule that an adulterous woman is sexually forbidden both to her husband and to her lover after the incident. Some couples can find the way to stay married after an affair. There is, in fact, a famous lover who modeled the potential to overcome the hurt and violation of infidelity, one from whom we can learn about marital forgiveness.

That lover was God.

In the theological imagination of the classical prophets of Israel, the relationship between God and the Jewish people was seen as a marriage. *Zaharti hesed n'urayikh, ahavat k'lulotayikh, lekhtekh aharay bamidbar, b'eretz lo z'ruah:* "I accounted to your favor the devotion of your youth, your love as a bride—how you followed me in the wilderness, in a land not sown," the prophet Jeremiah said (Jeremiah 2:2). In the prophetic construct, God was the groom, Israel the bride; Mt. Sinai was the *huppah*, the wedding canopy; the Torah was the *ketubbah*, the Jewish wedding contract; the forty-year period of wandering in the wilderness was the honeymoon. Not exactly like honeymooning in Hawaii or Club Med, to be sure, but when you are in love, even the Sinai Peninsula can be paradise.

If the time of wandering in the wilderness was the honeymoon, the time of settling the Land of Israel was like building a marriage. In Jerusalem, God and the Jewish people built a house: the *Beit Hamikdash*, the Holy Temple. They went about their business of building a life, of earning a living, of establishing a home, of raising a family. But something went wrong. Israel went astray, whoring after other gods. Canaanite practices were adopted. Local pagan gods were worshiped. Idolatry was a seductive force, inserting itself between God and the people. In the eyes of the prophets, this idolatry was the greatest sin, tantamount to theological adultery.

There were consequences for adultery. The First Temple was destroyed by the Babylonians in 586 B.C.E. The leaders of the Jews were either killed or taken into exile to Babylonia. Separation, despair, depression, and distance now defined the relationship between God and the Jewish people.

This theology was still operative some eight centuries later, when the Rabbis were creating the Talmud. Twenty pages of the talmudic tractate called *Gittin*, which deals with the delivery of the *get*, the bill of divorcement, tells stories surrounding the destruction of the Second Temple by the Romans and the loss of Jewish sovereignty in the year 70 C.E. What does that experience have to do with divorce, and why would it be in *Gittin*? Because if the moment of Sinai was the symbolic marriage, as the prophets taught, then the destruction of the Temple and the exile from our land was a symbolic divorce. After the adulterous worship of other gods, God's actions feel very much like a divorce.

But there was something unique about the way God divorced us. In God's experience, separation is only temporary, designed to teach a lesson and necessary to allow space between lovers for anger to subside. After a while, the separation is over. There is reconciliation, and there is forgiveness, and there is love. Scar tissue will form over the deep wounds caused by the infidelity. The relationship will endure, albeit changed: less naïve, less innocent, less pure. This was the message of hope and love delivered in the sixth century B.C.E. by the prophet Isaiah. In the following speech, Isaiah portrayed God speaking to the community that recently returned to Israel from the Babylonian exile after the destruction of the First Temple in 586 B.C.E.—a community that was still traumatized, devastated, depressed, and feeling alienated from God. Isaiah used the metaphor of marriage and divorce to illustrate the enduring relationship between God and Israel:

> Thus said the Lord: Where is the bill of divorce of your mother whom I dismissed? And which of My creditors was it to whom I sold you off?... For a little while I forsook you, but with vast love I will bring you back. In slight anger, for a moment, I hid My face from you; but with kindness everlasting I will take you back in love, said the Lord your Redeemer (Isaiah 50:1; 54:7–8).

God's anger and hurt and pain are real, to be sure, but God's love is eternal. God's mercy is infinite. God's forgiveness is not withheld. We learn from God that it is possible to survive an affair, to get beyond it, to sustain a relationship even after the ultimate affront. If it is possible to forgive your spouse for the infidelity, it would be acting in a way that is Godlike.

If you can see the adultery committed by your spouse as being a symptom of a bad relationship and not the cause of it; if you can understand infidelity as a red flag, a pathetic cry for attention, then you might be able to forgive it. If you can put the hurt and the humiliation behind you, then you might be able to live with the emotional and psychic scars and rebuild the relationship anew.

But humans, after all, are not God and are not expected to maintain a relationship that is based on trust when that trust has been shattered. Unlike God, our ways are not perfect, our love is conditional, our forgiveness is not absolute.

Whether or not you stay in your marriage after your spouse has had an affair depends on your level of tolerance for the pain and humiliation that results when your spouse has been unfaithful, and whether the benefits of staying in this relationship and rebuilding trust outweigh the burden of the hurt you feel. If you can get beyond the feelings of rejection, abandonment, betrayal, and heartache, you might be able to make your marriage work again.

ACKNOWLEDGING THE LONELINESS

Every marriage hits a crisis point. It might strike suddenly, without warning, as the result of a single event; it might evolve over time, when the realization finally hits that a gulf has opened between the two of you. But crisis is part of the process of marriage.

If ever it is safe to speak in generalizations, it is for this: every marriage has periods when the passion is gone, when the routine of daily life has made you numb. Even lovemaking, if it happens at all, is rote, as if neither one of you is fully present in the moment. And this happens in healthy marriages.

Crisis hits when you realize something profound is missing from your marriage, that some deep-seated need is not being met, that some unarticulated desire will never be fulfilled, that marriage has not fulfilled its promise of overcoming existential aloneness.

Crisis hits when you confront the reality that the partner you have chosen is not perfect. And even though we know in theory that no one is perfect, living with less than perfection in our spouses means that part of our soul will remain untouched, unknown, unloved by that person.

A man once told me of the fatherly advice he gave each of his children as they were being married. He shared with them the secret of the longevity of his marriage. He told them not to expect to receive 100 percent of what they hoped and wanted and desired from their spouses, that they should be satisfied with getting 80 percent of what they wanted and needed. If they did this, they would live a long life of marital bliss.

What this father was telling his children was that to expect to receive from marriage everything they wanted was unrealistic, unreasonable, and unwise. He was telling them that to hope that a single person could meet all of their needs was to set themselves up for radical disappointment and loneliness.

It should only be so simple.

Even using the 80/20 model, quite often people will focus on the 20 percent that is missing rather than on the 80 percent they receive. Once the positives of the 80 percent become routine, we accommodate them, taking them for granted, and reducing their statistical value. The equation goes out of balance, and the 20 percent seems like 100 percent. Unhappiness results. When that happens, there is trouble in paradise.

One mother shared with me the excitement she felt during the shopping outing to buy her son his suit for his Bar Mitzvah. She realized as they went from store to store what this suit symbolized to her: her son's coming of age, making the transition from a child to a young man. While her son was still *in utero* she had visions of him standing in front of a congregation as a Bar Mitzvah, chanting the ancient prayers, delivering his speech, beginning the process of becoming a man like so many other Jewish boys before him. She was flooded with memories—of the baby on the changing table, of the toddler in the playpen, of the toothless second-grader, of the boy who broke his arm playing soccer. And now, as she watched her son standing in his suit in front of the tailor's mirrors in the store, she was filled with the love and the joy and the *nachas* experienced by every mother of a Bar Mitzvah. Her eyes involuntarily filled with tears of happiness—tears that turned in an instant to tears of sadness.

She looked at her husband and understood by the look on his face that the experience of buying the Bar Mitzvah suit for their son held none of the emotions that she was feeling. As far as her husband was concerned, they were merely buying a suit.

Her husband wasn't Jewish. He didn't share the cultural and religious associations to the Bar Mitzvah experience that she felt. He couldn't possibly understand what she was feeling. For him, it was just a suit. Period.

And in the fifteen years of her marriage, she had never felt such loneliness. For the first time she realized that the man who fulfilled so many of her needs and wants and desires was not really her partner. At the moments when we feel like this, we feel emotionally unsupported, rejected, even abandoned. We wonder why we married this partner in the first place, and whether it wasn't a mistake. She admitted to me that for the first time in her marriage, she thought of divorce.

But there is a deeper issue with the 80/20 equation constructed by the father who spoke of it to me. I can't help but wonder how this father does his calculus. How does he calculate the statistics? How does he lay out the spreadsheet? Which part of our complex matrix of needs will go ignored, and will ignoring them be the cause of loneliness? Which part of our soul will be unloved?

Are all needs created equal?

What Can Adam Teach Us About Loneliness?

In the second chapter of the biblical Book of Genesis, Adam was created alone. After placing Adam in the Garden of Eden, God discovered that Adam was lonely.

> "It is not good for man to be alone," God said. So God created the animals as companions to Adam, to keep him company—perhaps as pets, perhaps as beasts of burden, perhaps as objects of fascination—but clearly different from Adam and lower on the scale of Creation. Adam was no longer alone on the planet.
>
> But that was not sufficient to overcome his loneliness. Even being God's partner was not enough; Adam still felt alone. Adam was in need of relationship.

A rabbinic discussion of this story imagines what it must have been like for Adam as the animals were paraded before him to receive their names from Adam. Adam noticed that the goose had its gander, the sheep had its ram, the cow had its bull. In a sad, wistful, pitiful voice, Adam said to God, "Every one has a partner, but I have none."

God had anticipated that God would be Adam's partner, but God was mistaken. Adam needed someone of his own species—a gender opposite—in order to feel connected on a deep spiritual level and to experience intimacy. Adam needed to touch and be touched, to experience sexual union, to long for the embrace of another. He needed the warmth of another body. Intimacy with God is different from the intimacy we experience with another human being. It was then that Eve was created.

> So the Lord God cast a deep sleep upon the man; and, while he slept, God took one of his ribs and closed up the flesh at that spot. And the Lord God fashioned the rib that God had taken from the man into a woman; and God brought her to the man (Genesis 2:21–22).

When Adam saw Eve for the first time, he said one of the most romantic things in all of biblical literature—perhaps in all of literature:

> Then the man said,
> "This one at last
> Is bone of my bones
> And flesh of my flesh.
> This one shall be called Woman,
> For from man was she taken."
> Hence a man leaves his father and his mother and clings to his wife,
> so that they become one flesh (Genesis 2:23–24).

Contrary to a popular notion, Eve was not created merely to provide a womb for the promulgation of the species. Eve was created to be in a relationship with Adam, to complement and complete Adam, to be a source and an object of companionship, warmth, tenderness, support, affection, and intimacy with another. The purpose of creating Eve, and hence the purpose of marriage, is to become one flesh.

Admittedly, the imagery here is decidedly masculine, but it is an image that can be embraced by women as well. Freud wrote of sex, for the man, as being a subconscious desire to return to the womb. In the Bible, sex is the conscious desire to return to the rib, to return to the primordial time when Man and Woman shared the same body. It is one of the gifts of God that the female sex organs are internal and the male organs are external, that one fits into the other. When physical intimacy is achieved within a relationship founded on a mutuality of respect, dignity, trust, exclusivity, and holiness, spiritual intimacy is achieved as well. As the Midrash tells it, when this happens we feel as if two halves of the same soul are reunited into a single whole.

According to the Torah, the need for intimacy is as essential to the soul as food and shelter are to the body. And it is in marriage that we fulfill that need.

Much of the time.

If the essential character of the human being is to be lonely, there is no greater loneliness than being in a marriage that has no intimacy. We begin our marriages with the hope and expectation that we will be able to give and get love, that we will touch and be touched, that we will nurture growth and be nurtured in return. But when you find yourself in a marriage that feels like two parallel lives that never intersect, in which two lovers become distant roommates, in which the presence of the other is a constant reminder that our loneliness is not going to be overcome in this marriage, the loneliness is heightened and made more painful. There is no escaping the pain—not in work, not in play, not in hours in the gym, not in a hundred seasons of Sunday morning football, not in a thousand pints of Häagen Dazs.

The ghosts of marital loneliness visit nightly, a constant reminder of a love lost. "When love was strong," a second-century sage remarked about his relationship with his wife, "we could have made our bed on a sword-blade; now that our love has grown weak, a bed of sixty cubits [roughly 90 feet] is not large enough for us" (*Sanhedrin* 7a). How many times I have heard described how husbands and wives sleep each night on the edge of their mattress, the gap between them more than just the unused mattress that separates them. Night after night they face the silent torture, never touching, never cuddling, never talking softly to each other in the quiet of the night: two silhouettes lying silent in the darkness, aching for the touch of the love of their youth, a touch that never comes.

Night after night they toss and turn, unable to close their eyes until fatigue and exhaustion bring sleep. Some nights are spent in a silent rage, screaming in that internal voice that is heard only inside the head, questioning, wondering, asking: "What is the matter with him? Why doesn't he touch me? Why doesn't he talk to me?" Or, "Why doesn't she stop nagging? Why is she not sexual?" And then finally, after countless nights of accusing the spouse of being inadequate, of rehearsing the litany of the wounds he inflicted on us, of listing all of the ways she has failed us, concluding the inevitable: "It isn't me. It must be him. He is incapable of loving." "She is selfish. She is a shrew."

Other nights are spent staring at the ceiling, questioning, wondering, asking: "Is it me?" And then finally, after countless nights of asking the question, concluding the inevitable, internalizing the answer, believing: "It is me. It must be me. I must be unlovable."

If I read the story of Adam and Eve in the Torah correctly, God does not intend for us to spend our lives with someone with whom intimacy is not possible. God did not create us to live with chronic loneliness, believing in our hearts that we are unworthy of love. This is not God's plan for us. This is not how God sees us. Even God understands that this lack of intimacy is not a healthy marriage, that God's vision of a holy union has not been fulfilled.

What Do You Do Now?

But having said all that we have said in this chapter about issues that justify divorce, we need to underscore that divorce should be the final resort. It is crucial that the threat of divorce not be used as a blunt instrument with which to hurt, or as a means of manipulating the other. There are steps that need to be taken before lawyers are consulted and someone moves out.

The first step is to be honest about a problem as it begins to develop. Denial needs to be resisted. Avoidance cannot continue. Truth must be faced. Conversations must take place between the two of you that include a description of how you feel, of what hurts, of what is missing for you in the marriage, of what you need from the other. And you must be prepared to listen to your spouse as much as you want your partner to listen to you.

The second step is to consult a rabbi. A rabbi will be able to help you sort out your feelings, to separate the psychological issues from the spiritual ones, to talk to you about the expectations of God as understood by Jewish tradition, to raise further issues for you to think about. If you belong to a synagogue, you already have a relationship with a rabbi; if you don't, now is a very good time to seek out a rabbi and affiliate with a synagogue.

The third step is to find the services of a qualified therapist and to be open to doing the work of therapy. Therapy has no usefulness to an unwilling client. Therapy should include individual counseling, couples counseling, or both. Finding the right therapist can be time-consuming, and it may take visits to three or four or twelve different therapists before the right therapist is found. The relationship between therapist and client is often like dating; a certain chemistry must exist between them for therapy to be effective. Your rabbi will be happy to recommend a few therapists, as will your friends who have had positive experiences. Do not be afraid or ashamed to ask people for references, for that is the best way of finding a therapist. The earlier therapeutic intervention takes place, the more likely the possibility that insight can be gained and strategies developed to deal with the issues between the couple.

The fourth step is to have patience. There is much therapeutic work to be done. Problems that took years to develop are not settled and solved overnight. You have years of your lives invested in each other, and patterns of behavior that are deep-seated do not change quickly. Do not give up easily. You have traveled a long path together and have a shared marital legacy that defines much of who you are. There was something in the character of your partner that caused you to fall in love with him or her in the first place. You need to do your best to try to find that something again, to uncover those special qualities that you once found endearing and worthy of your love.

But that is not always possible.

When all is said and done, the decision to divorce is the decision to exchange one pain for another. It is deciding that the loneliness in the marriage is greater than it would be out of it. It is deciding that trust has been shattered and cannot be restored. It is deciding that the one life we are given will be unfulfilled, and our full potential will never be realized, if we stay in this marriage.

At the end of the day, after all the talking and counseling and self-examination and bargaining and exploring and negotiating, one decides to divorce when the pain of disappointment is unbearable, when the emotional disconnect is irreparable, when the thought of living out the rest of one's days in brokenness and sadness and emptiness is unacceptable. If and when that point is reached, it is time to recognize that this relationship has come to an end, this marriage has run its course, and life needs to enter a new phase.

3

The Guilt Question: Is Divorce Kosher?

When David visited me, I understood that he had come to his rabbi because at the very core of his soul he was feeling guilty for having moved out of his house. The guilt he felt was visceral, enduring, emotionally crippling, and deeply religious, as if he had offended God's most basic sensibilities. The counseling he sought was spiritual.

He needed to be right with God.

"Be fruitful and multiply," God tells Adam and Eve as God marries them in the Garden, forever binding the act of procreation with the institution of marriage. According to a famous rabbinic legend, God is the rabbi performing the marriage rites, and the angels are the witnesses to the marriage. Under the wedding canopy, God tells Adam and Eve to be fruitful and multiply. These are the first words the first couple hears, at the very beginning of the human story. And they are among the first words that Noah and his sons hear as they come out of the Ark, when the world begins again after the devastation of the Flood.

In the biblical worldview, propagation of the species is not simply a biological impulse, a subconscious urge to participate in natural selection. Having children is a holy act, framed in the context of a divine command. Giving birth is the very first mitzvah in the Torah, and it is fulfilled within marriage. Human beings are neither fully creatures, like the animals, nor fully divine, like the angels, but an amalgam of both.

There are three equal partners in the birth of a child, our sages insist: the father, the mother, and God. Each partner has a role to play in the creation of life. Each makes a contribution to the uniqueness of the child; each has responsibility to raise this child. Although procreation is not the primary goal of marriage, nevertheless, because of the potential of creating life, getting married is a holy act. One of the words for marriage in Hebrew is *kiddushin,* which means "holiness." God, the source of all that is holy, calls us to sanctify the sexual union, to celebrate the mystery of sexual fidelity, to join our physical selves with another to create a spiritual whole. In the biblical understanding of coupling, therefore, getting married, having children, and raising families make human beings as close to God-like as they can be.

And here, in a nutshell, is David's problem: If marriage is a holy act, what does that make divorce?

David felt what most people feel when deciding to terminate a marriage: we are a divine disappointment. In terminating our marriages we have let God down. This feeling is universal. It exists, I have discovered, even in people who don't consider themselves to be religious. Divorce is a *shonda*, an embarrassment for the family and the community, a source of shame. This is not, we believe, what God wants of us: to terminate our marriages. This is not what God anticipated when we stood together under the marriage canopy.

David felt unable to look God in the eye. What would God say to David before the throne of judgment? Would God think David was a failure, a personal defeat, a sinner?

David was certain when he came to my office that I, as a representative of the Tradition, was going to tell him that what he had done was wrong. He was certain that I, as a rabbi, was going to tell him that Judaism believes in marriage until death do you part. David expected to hear that moving out of the house was a sin, and he wanted to hear from me ways to expiate that sin.

I didn't tell David what he expected me to say. But David was not to blame for his assumptions; he had been given the message over and over again that he was a sinner, as if this were a certain fundamental Jewish truth that everyone should know.

Why Do Jews Think Divorce Is a Sin?

When I was struggling with the question of my own divorce, I, like David, wanted to know what guidance, what wisdom I could glean from religious experts. One of the first books to which I turned was *Jewish Divorce Ethics: The Right Way to Say Goodbye* by Rabbi Reuven Bulka. Rabbi Bulka, with a Ph.D. in psychology, is one of the luminaries of modern Orthodox Judaism. He is a prolific author, who has written numerous books and articles on life's ultimate questions: love, marriage, divorce, death, the meaning of life.

As someone suffering the pain and confusion of going through a divorce, I found much of *Jewish Divorce Ethics* to be preachy, judgmental, at times painful, and ultimately disappointing. It felt to me as if the book had been written by a rabbi who had not experienced divorce and therefore could not fully understand the inner life of those who go through it. One passage from the beginning of the book, I trust, will suffice to illustrate. Rabbi Bulka writes:

> A radical shift in attitude has unfolded over the past few decades, away from saving marriages and towards saving individuals within the marriage. For example, the well-known consultant for the public, Abigail Van Buren, under her "Dear Abby" column, was asked relatively recently why it is that previously she would counsel couples to do all they can to save their marriages, but now she gives the impression that divorce could be the answer. She responded that it was more important to save people than to save marriages. She went on to explain

> that sometimes, in an effort to save a marriage not worth saving, people have destroyed themselves and each other.
>
> This response reflects the reality of contemporary times. Individual well-being, the right to self-realization, me-first, narcissistic ethic that has spread over the free world has also spilled over into the Jewish community. Rabbis today would be hard pressed in arguing such notions as "the importance of family harmony" or "maintaining the peace," to couples who are not getting along and bent on divorce (Bulka, *Jewish Divorce Ethics,* 1992, pp. 7–8).

I found these words to be enormously painful, giving expression as they do to what so many people believe: divorce is a result of the selfishness, narcissism, and individualism that constitute the disease of contemporary Western civilization. Rabbi Bulka suggests elsewhere in the book that couples today decide to dissolve their households simply because their marriages are "less than exciting." He writes as if divorce is a decision arrived at cavalierly, without the slightest attention to its consequences, as if the partners in the marriage are adolescents incapable of adult decisions.

I am certain Rabbi Bulka was unaware at the time he wrote those words just how damaging they could be to someone going through a divorce. What is more, I hope to show that Judaism takes a different position altogether in its evaluation of divorce.

Rabbi Bulka writes as if the institution of marriage is to be valued over individuals, as if the marriage is independent of the people in it. He appears to suggest that marriage is an entity unto itself, somehow more than the sum of its parts. He writes as if society has a greater stake in the percentage of intact marriages than in the psychological health of families and the people who populate them.

While it is true that some marriages that end in divorce could have been saved with earlier intervention and more effective counseling, to suggest that every terminated marriage was ended cavalierly is cruel. Not every marriage should remain intact. And not every marital problem has a solution. Sometimes we have to admit that it is better for everyone involved for some marriages to be dissolved. As we will see, the Torah understands this.

Divorce as a Disease

I soon discovered that Rabbi Bulka is not the only rabbi to promote this view that a marriage should stay intact at all costs. A couple came into my office to prepare for their wedding, the second marriage for both of them. Jewish law requires that before officiating at a second marriage, the rabbi must see documentary evidence of the religious dissolution of the first marriage.

Even more painful and more baffling for me to read than Rabbi Bulka's words was the cover letter that accompanied the document, testifying that this woman had in fact received her *get* and was free to marry. This woman had obtained her *get* shortly after the conclusion of the civil judgment dissolving her first marriage.

The couple sat quietly as I read the documentation of the religious divorce. They examined my face for reaction, hoping I would not find anything objectionable that would prevent their marriage from proceeding.

I did find something objectionable, and it probably showed on my face, but it had nothing to do with the efficacy of their religious divorce and everything to do with the attitude of the officiating rabbi.

The cover letter, written by the head of the rabbinical court supervising the religious divorce, was addressed to "Mrs. Schwartz."

The woman was addressed as Mrs., as if neither the civil nor the religious divorce had ever taken place:

> After speaking with you I regret to say that I am sorry I wasn't involved from the beginning. If I had, perhaps I would have been able to proscribe [sic] effective medicine to cure what ailed you both at the time. Different doctors proscribe [sic] different remedies to different patients. However, I know for a fact

> that my medicine is not only very potent but very effective. And knowing the both of you, I am certain that something could have been done to save the marriage.
>
> I realize that you are divorced, but I also know of many cases where divorced couples have come back together and the marriage was stronger than before. Their commitment to family and a reaching of better understanding was all that was necessary to make their renewed marriage successful.
>
> Mrs. Schwartz, so long as you do not remarry, you are still able to get back together under the "Chuppah." And until then, we hope and pray for you and your children's happiness.

I have no doubt that the author of this letter was coming from a place of deep concern, compassion, sympathy, even love. I have no doubt that this rabbi had the best interests of this woman and her ex-husband at heart. And I have no doubt that this rabbi was completely unaware of the insulting and painful effect of these words.

What was he thinking?

I don't know for sure, but my hunch is that he was conflicted about his role as the head of a rabbinical court whose task it is to terminate marriages. Knowing the interest of religion in promoting stable and fulfilling marriages as the primary arena for the expression of religious life—not to mention as the basic unit of social cohesion—he needed to distance himself from his work as the rabbi who supervised religious divorces. My hunch is that he wanted to see himself in the role of Aaron, Moses' brother and the first High Priest, who is credited by Tradition with having personally saved many marriages. Aaron is held up as a religious model to be emulated by subsequent generations of religious leaders. Hence this rabbi's sincere belief that his role was to encourage and facilitate a reconciliation between two incompatible and hostile former spouses.

I found the wording and tone of the letter to be patronizing and paternalistic. He wrote as if he knew better than the couple how they should live their lives, as if he held the magic bullet to end relationship difficulties, as if they were incapable and inadequate to figure this out for themselves.

Moreover, he spoke of divorce as a disease, as a terminal illness. Had they only come to him at the time their union began to hemorrhage, their marriage would not have died. He, the rabbinic doctor, the surgeon of record, had the cure. Their folly was in not consulting with him sooner.

One day, I trust, religious leaders will not view divorcees as being sick. They will see them as being divorced.

Finally, the rabbi insinuated that she had failed in her marriage because she and her ex-husband did not have a commitment to family. This he writes to the mother of five children.

Is Divorce Evil?

One final attitudinal example from writings of religious leaders suggesting that divorce is a sin. In 1968, the Jewish Federation in New York sponsored a symposium on Jews and divorce. This is how one of the presenters, a psychologist and professor of biblical literature and religious education, articulated the Jewish idea of divorce as framed in Jewish law:

> Divorce is antithetical to marriage and to the stable family that religion and state strive toward. But it is a way out for the inviolable, free individual who feels that he wants to or must break the marriage agreement. The individual is regarded as too sacred to suffer violation. Jewish law perceives man as a holy creature endowed with freedom of choice. Therefore, when all avenues of marital cohesion were employed and failed, and marriage is to be dissolved, divorce becomes a *necessary evil* to be accepted (Menahem M. Brayer, *Jews and Divorce,* pp. 13–14; emphasis mine).

Even in a sympathetic presentation of divorce, where the author writes that the option of divorce is available to couples suffering in a loveless marriage, divorce is described as a necessary evil. The term "evil" is loaded with moral judgment.

We can look back at the twentieth century and define evil. Adolf Hitler was evil. Pol Pot was evil. Ethnic cleansing was evil.

Is divorce to be included in this litany?

In this religious climate, is it any wonder that David felt he was committing a sin?

There are too many examples of such ideas for the opinions of these clergy to be a coincidence. Is the idea that divorce is a sin the opinion of Judaism? Do these rabbis—and all the rabbis who write and preach and teach the idea that divorce is a sin—represent traditional Judaism? Or is this a newfound religious ethic responding to a social phenomenon that did not previously exist, namely, the enormous prevalence of divorce that we find in the modern world?

WHAT DOES JUDAISM *REALLY* BELIEVE?

What does Judaism believe? What does God believe? Is divorce a sin?

The answer, as we shall see, is "no." Divorce is painful, it is tragic, it is certainly heartbreaking. But it is not a moral infraction.

The procedure in the Talmud for divorce is established in the Bible:

> A man takes a wife and possesses her. She fails to please him because he finds something obnoxious about her, and sends her away from his house; she leaves his household and becomes the wife of another man; then this latter man rejects her, writes her a bill of divorcement, hands it to her, and sends her away from his house; or the man who married her last dies. Then the first husband who divorced her shall not take her to wife again, since she has been defiled—for that would be abhorrent to the Lord. You must not bring sin upon the land that the Lord your God is giving you as a heritage (Deuteronomy 24:1–4).

This biblical passage speaks as if the institution of divorce preceded this biblical discussion. It is apparent that divorce was a preexisting legal remedy for the termination of marriage; otherwise, this entire passage makes little sense. Deuteronomy presumes the fact of divorce; these verses are concerned primarily with the prohibition against the remarriage of a divorced couple if the wife married another man subsequent to the first divorce. Deuteronomy speaks about the procedure of divorce only indirectly, suggesting that divorce as a legal institution is rooted in ancient custom and not prescribed by biblical law. The instrument of a bill of divorcement predates Deuteronomy, which scholars claim was written at the end of the seventh century before the Common Era.

The remarriage of a divorced couple under these conditions is abhorrent to the Lord; the divorce, apparently, is not. Discussion of the institution of divorce—its content, its moral stature, its procedure—is surprisingly absent in the Bible. Not a word of judgment, not a hint of opinion, neither an expression of condemnation nor one of reassurance.

Which leaves us to ask: even if divorce is permitted, is it kosher? Is divorce an option for good people? What does God really think?

Some point to Malachi 2:16 as a clear indication of God's mind, in which God says quite simply, "'I detest divorce' says the Lord, the God of Israel." Reading this, one might easily conclude that God does not want to allow divorce under any conditions. But this phrase cannot be understood in isolation. When taken in context, what the prophet is talking about in this section is not a blanket condemnation of the institution of divorce. Instead, Malachi delivers a blistering rebuke of the practice of his contemporary Israelite men who divorced their Israelite wives, the wives of their youths, and married non-Israelite women. In other words, what God detests in this instance is intermarriage, not divorce *per se*. And this only makes sense. After all, if God did not want divorce at all, would the Torah permit divorce?

The passage in Deuteronomy is sparse in its discussion of divorce. Deuteronomy does not delineate specific conditions for divorce: No parameters of acceptable and unacceptable grounds for divorce, no discussion of the role of women in divorce, no description of the bill of divorcement, no procedure for the writing and delivery of the bill of divorcement. But that there is divorce, and that divorce was a fact of life from the earliest of times, is clear.

WHAT DOES THE TALMUD SAY?

The Talmud is the central text of rabbinic civilization. It contains a wealth of material reflecting the daily life of communities that spanned nearly seven hundred years, from the second century before the Common Era until the end of the fifth century of the Common Era. It was composed in the lands of Israel and in Babylonia by the classical architects of the brand of Judaism we live today. All study of Judaism as a religious system must begin with an examination of the teachings of the Talmud, for the religion of Judaism we live today is talmudic, not biblical. Much of the wisdom that inheres in Jewish tradition can be found in its pages. In the Talmud, a work of antiquity, can be found much truth that is eternal and speaks to the hearts and minds of our generation.

The Talmud is the way the rabbinic sages read the Bible.

It remained to the Rabbis of the talmudic age to flesh out the laws of divorce. And flesh out they did. They discussed the conditions for valid and invalid *gittin*. They explored the rules of agency in delivering the *get* and the rules of witnessing the signing and delivery of the *get*. They created a conditional *get*, as for example, a *get* given to a woman by her husband when he went off to war. The conditional *get*, effective retroactively, provided a remedy for the agonizing problem that existed when a husband failed to return from battle and there were no witnesses who could testify to his death or produce the remains of his body. In the absence of proof of the husband's death, the wife would be unable to marry another. With the conditional *get*, she became a divorcee. The Rabbis of the Talmud, in confronting the complexities of life, expanded the rules of divorce far beyond the discussion in the

Torah. Their talmudic discussions are intricate, deep, complex, creative, and thoughtful.

It is remarkable, therefore, that the Rabbis of the Talmud tell us much about *gittin*, but they don't tell us much about divorce. Not, that is, until the very last page of Tractate *Gittin*. The discussion of the propriety of divorce is postponed until the very last moment.

Perhaps the sages didn't want to talk about divorce either.

Before we venture any deeper into their discussions, a quick word of recognition about the nature of their social, intellectual, and religious world and how it differs from ours is appropriate. In the first to the sixth centuries of the Common Era, the leadership of the religious community was universally male. The discussions found in the Talmud are almost always from the perspective of the male. In our age, no discussion about marriage and divorce would proceed along those lines because our sensibilities are so much different from theirs. Our cultural assumptions have changed—and for the better, I hasten to add. Most of us understand gender roles in today's society as essentially egalitarian, and the procedure for divorce, first established in the Torah and expanded in the Talmud, is not egalitarian. Men have a disproportionate amount of power as a result. Nevertheless, if we can suspend the gender difficulties for the sake of this discussion, there is much to be learned about divorce from the wisdom of our ancestors, and I argue that we ignore their discussions at our own peril.

The Rabbis were rarely unanimous in their opinions. One is not surprised to find a difference of opinion among the ancient Rabbis regarding divorce. They argued about almost everything. One cannot turn a page of Talmud without seeing disagreement and argumentation, so to find differences regarding a matter of such critical social importance is to be expected. This particular disagreement is early, as rabbinic tradition goes. It dates from the first century of the Common Era. The debate is recorded as one of the points of contention that raged between two schools of rabbinic scholars: the House of Shammai and the House of Hillel. Tradition follows the opinion of the House of Hillel, for we are the religious heirs of this school. Some time in the first century, the Hillelites gained ascendancy. To their credit, they recorded the opinions of their adversaries, the Shammaites, allowing us a glimpse into their intellectual world.

THE HOUSE OF SHAMMAI VERSUS THE HOUSE OF HILLEL: WHAT IS OBNOXIOUS?

The differences between these two schools emerged from the cultural and religious assumptions each school brings to the reading of the biblical text. Two different ways to read the biblical text; two different conclusions regarding God's intentions and desires. Let us enter their debate about divorce.

We begin with the opinion of the House of Shammai. Deuteronomy gives the reason for the separation and the termination of the marriage in obscure, ambiguous, unclear terms: "She fails to please him because he finds something obnoxious about her." The translation "because he finds something obnoxious about her" is a modern one; this translation, as we shall see, is influenced by the conclusion of the debate between the two schools. However, the term translated as "obnoxious" in the original Hebrew is *ervat davar,* and it is on the meaning of these two Hebrew words that the entire debate hinges.

In the eyes of the House of Shammai, *ervat davar* can mean one thing and one thing only: the appearance of sexual infidelity. The suspicion of adultery on the part of the wife, therefore, is the only grounds for the dissolution of a marriage in Jewish law (if proven adultery was committed by the wife, the Bible provides the death penalty as a punishment). Short of the suspicion of adultery, the House of Shammai would not allow a couple to be divorced. Accordingly, this is the way the verse should be translated following the opinion of the House of Shammai:

> The House of Shammai say: "A man should not divorce his wife unless he has found her in some indecency *(ervat davar),* as

> it is said, because he has found some matter of indecency in her."

This understanding of *ervat davar* is perfectly reasonable. In the Book of Leviticus, the word *ervah* means just that: illicit sexuality. Short of unchastity, the Shammaites held, divorce is not permissible. The House of Shammai is apparently unmoved by relationship issues. Divorce is a punishment, a necessary consequence for a serious moral infraction.

Not so the House of Hillel. They read the same biblical verse as their colleagues in the House of Shammai, but as we can see, their interpretation is quite innovative:

> And the House of Hillel say, "Even if she burned his food, as it is said, because he has found something obnoxious *(ervat davar)* about her."

At first blush, the interpretation of the House of Hillel does violence to the biblical verse. What is the meaning of that enigmatic phrase, *even if she burns his food?* Did the House of Hillel mean this literally or metaphorically? Could the Hillelites really believe that the Torah would allow the dissolution of a marriage simply because the wife had a bad day in the kitchen? Could the Hillelites believe that marriage should be as easily terminated as an unsatisfactory magazine subscription?

Not likely. It is probable that "burning his food" was an idiomatic expression popular in the first century of the Common Era whose meaning was lost to subsequent generations. Whatever its original meaning, it is clear that the House of Hillel allows for a myriad of relationship issues to warrant the termination of a marriage. Whatever its original meaning, if the husband could contemplate divorce because of something as inconsequential as burning his food, he appears to be devoid of patience, without tolerance, bad-tempered. Everything she does is an irritant to him. Even the sound of her voice sets him on edge.

The House of Hillel believe that the Torah would not force this couple—or any couple—to remain imprisoned in a marriage that makes either of the partners miserable.

WHEN THE LOVE IS GONE

The Talmud immediately brings another opinion, one given a century after the debate between the House of Shammai and the House of Hillel. Following in the footsteps of the House of Hillel, Rabbi Akiba added another twist, a new wrinkle on the interpretation of *she fails to please him, because he finds something obnoxious about her:*

> Rabbi Akiba says, "Even if he found another prettier than she."

Rabbi Akiba, who lived in the beginning of the second century and was one of the primary architects of rabbinic Judaism, focused on the phrase "she fails to please him" to include what is arguably a more modern understanding of love and romance as being necessary for marriage. Rabbi Akiba said that even if he found another woman more desirable he has grounds for divorce.

Perhaps a marriage was an arranged one, and the husband and wife incompatible. Perhaps they were married when they were young, and they've now changed beyond recognition. Perhaps one or both of them did something unforgivable. We could conjecture until the end of time.

But of this we are sure: there is no magic in this fictitious marriage. There is no burning desire to be together. There is no longing for each other when they are apart. There is no mutuality of respect, no companionship, no sharing of hopes and dreams, no partnership in building a life together. This is not a marriage. This husband and wife are not in love.

Well, that is only half true. The husband is in love, but with another woman.

How often this story has played itself out in human history.

Rabbi Akiba demonstrated great humanity and compassion in his ruling. I like to believe that were Rabbi Akiba alive today, he would make the same ruling for a woman as he made for a man. It would be understandable to say to this man, to this couple, that marriage is a sacred obligation, that marriage is a lifelong commitment, that marriage is for better or for worse, till death do you part.

It would be understandable to repeat all the clichés, which we have heard so often, about no promises of rose gardens and the taking the good with the bad and the value of sacrifice.

It would be understandable, but it would be cruel.

It is cruel to require a husband and wife to live in a loveless marriage, and Rabbi Akiba does not require it. It is cruel to require them both to be unhappy, angry, bitter, disappointed in the way their lives have turned out. It is cruel to make them live the rest of their lives feeling trapped, unnurtured, unfulfilled. If marriage is the foundation of society, a painful marriage leads to a society in pain. It is not in society's interest to perpetuate this level of unhappiness.

Even Rabbi Akiba—whose own personal love story, shrouded in legend, is held by some as a model of the ideal romantic marriage—understood the pain of a loveless marriage and understood the place of divorce in society. For Rabbi Akiba, divorce is not a tragedy but a remedy. It is a decision to trade one pain for another: the pain of living in a loveless marriage for the pain of separation and loss. But choosing to divorce is to select the one pain of the two for which there is, ultimately, a healing.

Would that the spirit of Rabbi Akiba were alive today. Would that modern rabbis shared Rabbi Akiba's attitude toward divorce. Would that modern rabbis could learn to feel the anguish in the souls of those who go through divorce, and not make us feel that we are sinners, evil, selfish and narcissistic and less than human. There would be, in my judgment, far less unnecessary guilt—and yes, far less unhappiness.

That is not to say that the talmudic Rabbis advocated divorce; they most certainly did not. That is not to say that the talmudic Rabbis did not attempt to deter divorce as much as possible; they did. They tried to deter divorce because they understood how it could grow out of marital rage, and rage can subside. They tried to deter divorce because they understood the deep sadness of it. If a way to recreate marital harmony could be found, it must be sought. They understood the disappointment and the pain and the inner turmoil and the disruption of lives and communities that comes in the wake of divorce.

But they never considered divorce to be a sin.

WHEN GOD CRIES

The final word in the Talmud on divorce is given to Rabbi Eleazar, an earlier colleague of Rabbi Akiba. It is attitudinal, reserved for the very last page of the talmudic tractate that provides the legal parameters of religious divorce (*Gittin* 90b).

Rabbi Eleazar leaves us with a stunning poetic image:

> Rabbi Eleazar said: If a man divorces his first wife, even the altar sheds tears.

Rabbi Eleazar answers the question with which we began: Where is God in all this? Where is the holiness in divorce? It is easy to find holiness in a healthy marriage. It is easy to find holiness in the raising of children and the running of a household. But where is holiness in divorce? Where is God?

Rabbi Eleazar gives us an answer through the symbol of the altar. In the mythic structure of the Temple in Jerusalem, the altar was the point of contact between heaven and earth. Through the sacrificial service, the altar served as the point of intersection where God, who resided in the heavenly palace, connected with the physical world. At the altar the heavenly God was worshipped by God's earthbound children. The altar was a place of intimacy.

It is at the altar that God cries about divorce.

God cries about divorce not because God is judging us as sinners, as so many people believe. God cries not because God is disappointed in our failure, as so many rabbis teach. God cries because God, like us, is in pain and cries with us. When we hurt, God hurts. God is present in God's tears.

God does not abandon us when we go through difficult times. We are not left alone to fend for ourselves in the wilderness of loneliness. I was not alone through my divorce. I know that God was with me through my divorce because the Talmud teaches me that God cried with me. And there is holiness in those divine tears.

This is a God I can believe in. This is the God I do believe in.

4

The Psychological Question: What Do I Do with All This Anger?

"Heav'n has no Rage, like Love to Hatred turn'd; Nor Hell a Fury, like a Woman scorn'd," William Congreve wrote in *The Mourning Bride*, published in 1697. This phrase is a household cliché, known in some form to just about everyone who speaks English. It has been quoted and reworked by numerous authors who wanted to convey the mood of a woman on an emotional rampage at the end of a romance. Hell itself could provide no greater suffering.

In my experience, however, Congreve was only half right. Hell hath another fury besides a woman scorned, and that is the rage of a divorced man.

Anger knows no gender distinctions.

A constant companion of divorcing couples is anger and rage. Of all the emotions surrounding divorce, anger is the most destructive. Hardly a divorcing couple escapes anger's all-consuming demands. Anger is almost always a dark power in divorces; it has the irresistible control of an addiction.

As I was thinking about the role of anger in divorce, and trying to make sense of my own anger and emotional outbursts, I rented a video I had not seen since its premiere in 1989: *The War of the Roses.* I remembered the movie as being a comedic exaggeration about the divorce from hell.

The way I watched it this time was much different from a decade earlier.

One line in the movie puts a chill in my soul. When Barbara Rose, the wife, asks for a divorce, Oliver, the husband asks why. She responds, "Because when I watch you eat, when I see you asleep, when I look at you lately, I want to smash your face in."

Who among us who has ever been married hasn't felt this rage? Who among us who has ever been married hasn't felt the desire to smash in the face of the partner? It happens in every marriage. A rabbi once said to me, only half in jest, that in twenty-five years of marriage he hadn't once thought of divorce. He had thought of murder, but not divorce.

And then I learned that a rabbi in the Northeast had been indicted for allegedly hiring someone to kill his wife. The joke ceased to be funny.

The truth is that relationships often descend to mutually self-destructive behaviors. If rage is given free reign, and if relationships are allowed to hemorrhage, and if the damage is irreparable, and if former lovers become combatants, divorce, like war, is hell.

The War of the Roses is a story of what happens when anger has no master. As anger and disappointment morph into rage and fury, there are no limits, no boundaries, no end to anger's destructive force. It is a dark force that feeds on itself as it becomes a ravenous, insatiable monster, devouring everything and everyone in its path. *The War of the Roses* is a dark, deranged, psychotic narrative of modern divorce. And it touches exposed nerves.

On one level we know that the movie is the *reductio ad absurdum* of comic farce. On a deeper, more visceral level, however, the movie was disturbing because it touched on primal fears and anxieties of married people. Many people who watched the movie in the theatre stopped laughing because they recognized a certain truth most of us do not want to face.

Truth be told, there is a piece of Oliver and Barbara Rose in each of us, and that disturbs. This movie makes us feel vulnerable because we feel we are watching a part of ourselves, because we see our darkest subconscious on the screen. Each of us is capable of Rose-like behavior.

We'd like to believe that if we were in their situation, we would react in ways more civilized, more grownup, more healthy than these movie protagonists. We'd like to believe that we would be able to step back, take a breath, objectively assess our behavior, behave like adults.

But anger and rage are not about making sense. At the time of an enraged outburst during divorce, anger often leads us to destructive behaviors, making us feel that we need to get even, to exact revenge on the one who hurt us.

How Can I Punish My Ex?

One might think the story in this movie is an exaggeration until one reads news reports of estranged husbands who kidnap their children, or shoot their ex-wives, or worse.

I know of one woman who was so angry with her estranged spouse that she had the sheriff's deputies waiting for him in her driveway when he was late in bringing the children back from his court-scheduled visitation. The court agreement called for him to bring the children home at a specified hour. The sheriff's deputies arrested the father for violating his visitation agreement. His children watched as their father was put in handcuffs, placed in a sheriff's unit, and driven off to jail.

He was ten minutes late.

Often, divorcing couples will use their children as blunt implements with which to bludgeon their ex-spouses.

Another woman told me of a similar episode with her ex-husband. He was without a car. Their custody agreement was for her to pick up the two children at his apartment at the appointed hour when his visitation was over. One day, she went to his apartment at the designated time to retrieve the kids and found no one at home. She left, returning a few minutes later. Still no sign of the three of them, so she left once again. She returned a third time, and still her ex-husband was late. After three attempts to retrieve her children, she returned home, full of anger, determined that it was his problem to get the children home.

The children did make it home, escorted by one of Beverly Hills' finest. The father was so angry with his ex-wife for not picking up the children that he had called the police and accused his ex-wife of abandoning her children. The police drove the children home; the police were angry with the mom for not getting the children.

They lived only five blocks from each other.

The tragedy is that in punishing his ex-wife, the father used his children as the rod not to be spared. Calling the police was not the only option available to the father; he could have taken the children home in a taxicab, or sent them by themselves in the cab, or even walked them home.

But both parents had an agenda beyond just getting the boys home. Each wanted to hurt the other, to punish the other for some real or perceived wrong. They both believed they were the aggrieved parties, that they were in the right, that the other needed to be taught a lesson.

And what had they taught their children in the process?

I pray for the day when the police will be used only to solve crimes and not be called upon to navigate between sparring ex-spouses. No doubt this is not what the police department had in mind when choosing the slogan "to protect and to serve." And I pray for the day that children of divorce will be allowed to be children, with a childhood free from being in the middle of an adult battlefield.

These stories are not simply Hollywood fantasies. These are real stories about anger, hostility, and rage. Anger happens within all of us for some very good psychological reasons. And it is a mitzvah to understand why this happens within us when going through a divorce.

Where Does Anger Come From?

Anger is not a sign of weakness. Neither is anger the result of a deep-seated character flaw. Anger is the natural response to a real human condition. Richard Gardner, in his wonderful book *The Parents Book About Divorce*, identifies the cause of anger as "one in which the individual experiences frustration over an inability to remove an irritant." Frustration results from a lack of control, of an inability to bring about or influence a desired end.

Anger is a very human emotion. We know this because we find it in God. We find examples of God's anger throughout the Bible and the Talmud. Many of the stories and legends in the Talmud have as their goal the humanizing of God, making God more accessible to us by describing God in anthropomorphic terms. One of my favorite talmudic images of God is found toward the very beginning of the Talmud. It talks about a situation in which God's anger is aroused:

> Rabbi Yohanan said: Whenever the Holy One, blessed be He, comes into a Synagogue and does not find ten persons there, He immediately becomes angry, For it is said (Isaiah 50:2): "Why is it when I came there was no man? When I called, there was no answer?" (TB *Berakhot* 6b).

In this short yet remarkable statement by Rabbi Yohanan, God is portrayed in very human terms. In its original context, Isaiah's prophetic declaration was made to the members of the community living in Jerusalem in the immediate period after the building of the Second Temple in the sixth century B.C.E. Apparently, the Temple remained empty and abandoned in the beginning. God, in the words of the prophet, cried out in pain and isolation, expressing deep loneliness and alienation, inviting worshippers back into an intimate relationship. Centuries later, Rabbi Yohanan, living in a world in which there was no longer the Jerusalem Temple, recontextualized the prophetic verse so that it applied to the synagogue as well. Rabbi Yohanan asserted that when a congregation shows up to pray, God has already arrived at the synagogue, calling out to the worshippers, seeking the same feelings of intimacy and fellowship and companionship that we all crave.

The image of God that emerges from this teaching is that God, just like humans, is in need of community. God, just like humans, is in search of relationship. And just like humans, God expects to find that relationship in the synagogue. When God's plans are frustrated because not enough people are present, then God feels neglected, dismissed, rejected, abandoned, and lonely. God is hurt. God reacts just as you and I react to hurt, particularly the hurt that comes from being disappointed by someone we love: God gets angry.

One can almost imagine God, as it were, with neck veins popping out, brow furrowed, hands thrown up, pacing in an empty synagogue, voice raised to frightening heights. The portrait of God in this story is very human. This is an anger we all know.

There is a famous story about a husband and wife, married for a very long time, who had a son together in their old age. One morning the father got up early and, under the cover of darkness, took his son on a trip of considerable distance, a trip fraught with very real dangers. He neither consulted with nor informed his wife of his plans. The wife, apparently, was so angry with her husband that she left him.

That father was Abraham, the mother, Sarah. The son was Isaac, and we have heard this story before. But now we hear it from Sarah's point of view.

The *Akedah* narrative of Genesis 22 ends with Abraham returning to Beer Sheva, the place from where he had left, the place where he left Sarah. Chapter 23 begins immediately with the narrative of the death and burial of Sarah. When we last heard of Sarah, on the day when Abraham took Isaac on that trip, she was in Beer Sheva. When we meet up with her again, as Abraham goes to bury her and to mourn her, she is in Hevron. Between the beginning of the *Akedah* journey and the return, Sarah had left Abraham's tent. Sarah left Abraham, and at the time of her death, she was alone. She left him, and we can understand why. Abraham took her son, her only son, whom she loved, to kill him on the altar of Abraham's religious beliefs. The biblical text is silent about Sarah's emotional state at the time of the separation, but it is not difficult to project what she was feeling.

There was serious anger, relationship-destroying anger, pathological anger in the marriage of the first Patriarchs. Sarah was so angry that she could no longer speak to Abraham, could no longer live with him. They never spoke again, not even through lawyers.

If anger is a child of marriage, then anger is the midwife of divorce. Divorce is often born with anger and nursed on anger.

There are many irritants within relationships that result in anger, and many stimulants to anger throughout the separation and divorce process. All along the way there are time bombs waiting to detonate as decisions need to be made and positions are negotiated.

Anger in Divorce Can Be a Good Thing

But anger serves a valuable and necessary purpose in the divorce process, and it fulfills an enormous psychological function. The good news is this: anger that is understood, given healthy expression, and ultimately resolved provides a positive psychological catalyst toward transition, growth, insight, and acceptance. Paradoxically, as unpleasant and as uncomfortable and as ugly as it is, anger is a stage that everyone going through a divorce must endure.

Elisabeth Kübler-Ross changed the way we understand the psychological process of dying and grieving in her seminal study called *On Death and Dying*. Kübler-Ross isolated five distinct psychological stages a terminally ill patient and their loved ones pass through, from the moment of learning about the catastrophic illness until the final breath. She labeled the five stages denial, anger, bargaining, depression, and acceptance.

Those who experience the death of a relationship and the loss of a primary love object go through such a process. The process of divorce is, as we have said, a series of little deaths. The psychological process of divorce, in many ways, parallels grieving the loss of a loved one, but with one fundamental difference: in divorce, the one who has died to you is usually still in your life.

At some point in the marital relationship—in every marital relationship—one or both partners in the marriage evidences patterns of denial. We admit and acknowledge our hurt and disappointment and unhappiness for a moment, only to lapse back into denial in order to sustain the marriage. We are quick to see difficulties and deficiencies in the marriages of our friends and relatives. We even skillfully evaluate the problem and offer solutions to our friends who are suffering. But often when it comes to our own marriages, denial is a vicious master. "No, not me. I don't have a bad marriage. This isn't happening to me." Excuses are made for behaviors. Rationalizations are constructed. Denial is maintained until it can be maintained no longer.

And then, as disbelief turns to deep disappointment, the numbing properties of denial turn to the incendiary passions of anger. We inevitably get to the stage of anger—and with very good reason. There is much to be angry about.

WHY ARE WE ANGRY?

We become angry at not being loved. We become angry about the countless hurts and insults and abuses and indifferences inflicted over the years. Angry that he wasn't my father. Angry that she turned out not to be my mother. Or maybe she was. Angry that she is independent, with a life of her own, separate from me. Angry at feeling like a failure, that the years we have invested in each other, the "best years of our lives," were wasted. Angry that I have to start all over again. Angry at being abandoned. Angry at feeling betrayed. Angry at being rejected. Angry at him for not being the person I needed. Angry that life did not turn out the way it was planned.

Angry that the person who at one time couldn't live without me, can. And will.

There is much to be angry about. Anger is real, it is deep, it cuts to the bone. But feelings are neither good nor bad; they just are. And anger is.

Anger is, because one who is going through divorce is living through a death experience. Anger is, because without it, none of us would be able to grow through the experience.

What Do We Do with Our Anger?

Understanding the source of anger, however, is only the first step, albeit a large leap forward. The issue is, what do I do now that I know I'm going to be angry? And what do I do now that I know my ex-spouse is going to be angry?

This is the central question. It is an issue that transcends the immediacy of the divorce. Fundamentally, the issue is one of character. The issue is what kind of a person I am. It is during the stage of anger that one's character is fully tested. The *Zohar*, the primary text of Jewish mysticism, says that "When a man becomes angry, his true character becomes manifest" (*Zohar* II, 182b). Notice that the *Zohar* does not say "if" one becomes angry, but "when."

The Rabbis of the Talmud also understood anger to be a test of character. In a lovely aphorism, skillfully juxtaposing three words that share assonance, the second-century Palestinian sage Rabbi Ilai said that by three things a person is known.

The first word is *b'koso*, literally, his cup. How and when a person drinks, how a person handles alcohol, is a great barometer of a person's character. We learn a great deal about people at the office holiday party, or at social events, or at the corner bar by the frequency and volume of alcohol consumption and by the way people behave while inebriated.

The second word is *b'keeso*, his pocket. The way a person earns and spends money is one of the greatest indicators of his or her fundamental values and commitments. Money tells us a great deal about someone: Is this person cheap, frugal, selfish, or generous, philanthropic, giving?

The third word, finally, is *uv'kaaso*, his anger. One of the benchmarks of a person's character is the ease and frequency of visible anger. Habitual anger reflects a bitterness of the soul. One does not have to have gone to school with Freud to understand that someone who is bitter, overly pedantic, irascible, impatient, and quick to yell is an unhappy person. The external display of anger is an indication of an inner disequilibrium.

An angry person is dangerous to be around. The toxic words spoken in anger pierce the heart like flak through armored vehicles, leaving emotional casualties in their path.

A person going through a divorce is an unhappy person, and the anger of a person going through a divorce can be epic. But to inflict pain and hurt through angry words during a divorce is to fail the character test.

LETTING OUT ANGER IS IMPORTANT

The obvious question, of course, is this: how is destructive anger to be avoided? When the primitive urge to yell, to insult, to break something is overpowering, when adrenaline is pumping and behavior is beyond control, how does one not succumb to the ravages of rage?

Rage can be compared to fire. Fire can heat a home, cook our food, light our way; fire can destroy everything in its path, ravage in an instant, scar for life. Knowing how, when, and where to use fire is the difference, in many cases, between life and death.

California is blessed with beautiful rolling hills that are covered with trees as well as small growth and brush. Every summer, as the heat dries out the brush, there is the threat of devastating fires in the hills of southern California—a threat often realized. The Los Angeles Fire Department has a program of controlled burning to minimize the effects of these forest fires: certain areas are set on fire in order to burn away the small underbrush, which acts as kindling during the dry summer months. If this underbrush is burned away under controlled circumstances, the hills are less incendiary; the potential for a devastating fire is lessened. The firefighters, here in California as well as elsewhere around the country, use fire to prevent fire. A small fire prevents larger fires from raging out of control.

We have much to learn from firefighters.

Like controlled burning, anger must be let out in controlled measures, expressed honestly but not in ways that create scorched earth. The poet William Blake understood just this when he wrote:

> I was angry with my friend:
> I told my wrath, my wrath did end.
> I was angry with my foe:
> I told it not, my wrath did grow.

There are no shortcuts, and the only way beyond anger is through it. Anger that is suppressed, that is turned inward, becomes depression. Anger that is displaced becomes destructive, unreasonable, impossible to resolve; it is directed at people and objects that usually have nothing to do with the source of the anger—which often are our children. In order to get beyond anger, it must be articulated, embraced, and blessed.

We have much to learn from firefighters, and we have much to learn from God. It is at the stage of anger, when we are behaving in the least civilized manner, when the potential for destruction is absolute, that we have the opportunity to be the most human. And we become the most human when we become most like God.

How Can We Bless Anger?

A momentary digression:

An entire tractate in the Talmud discusses blessings—all kinds of blessings. Early morning blessings, late night blessings, blessings for eating and drinking, for experiencing wonders of nature, for going to the bathroom, for before and after travel—in short, blessings that cover the entire range of human experience. The purpose of these blessings is to instill a sense of gratitude, of wonder, of the mystery of being, of an awareness of God's enormous power in Creation. Life presents endless opportunities for blessings.

There are also blessings for history, blessings to be said when standing at a place where God entered into history and brought a miracle. The talmudic list is long: the Red Sea; the Jordan River; the rock that Moses sat on during the battle with Amalek, where victory was assured as long as he kept his hands raised; the walls of Jericho that came tumbling down; and so on. One who stands in the place where God made a miracle is given the following benediction to say:

> *Barukh sh'asah nisim la'avotaynu bamakom hazeh:* "Blessed is the one who made a miracle for our ancestors in this place."

However, a curious listing is included in the litany of places where miracles occurred. Included in this list are the names of Lot and his wife, as if "Lot and his wife" were a place, which they most certainly were not. You will remember that Lot, Abraham's nephew, chose to reside in the cities of the plain surrounding the Dead Sea. The largest of these cities were the infamous Sodom and Gomorrah, symbolic to this day of sin and evil and destruction.

What miracle was brought for Lot and his wife? Sodom and Gomorrah were destroyed in a devastating earthquake from below and fire from above. Can a blessing be said for death and destruction? Do we praise God for capital punishment?

There is no more devastating scorched earth policy than the narrative of the destruction of the biblical cities of Sodom and Gomorrah. God, in anger at the sins of the five cities of the plain, destroyed the cities in a great conflagration and upheaval, in a hail of fire and brimstone.

Still, in the midst of the fierceness and destruction, even in the midst of anger and devastating rage, God was able to bring a miracle. God saved Lot and his family, out of God's sense of justice and compassion and mercy.

Amar Rabbi Yohanan: Afilu b'shaat kaaso shel hakadosh barukh hu, even in the time of God's anger, Rabbi Yohanan tells us, *zokher et ha tzaddikim*, God remembers the righteous. How does Rabbi Yohanan know this? Because the Bible tells us this:

> Thus it was that, when God destroyed the cities of the plain and annihilated the cities where Lot dwelt, God was mindful of Abraham and removed Lot from the midst of the upheaval (Genesis 19:29).

According to the Rabbis of the Talmud, when we stand and look at the area of the plain in which the destruction took place, we are required to say a blessing. In this benediction we are required to remember God's power for both creation and destruction, for healing and for illness, for justice and for mercy. The words we are required to say on the shores of the Dead Sea are *Barukh zokher et hatzaddikkim*, blessed is the one who remembers the righteous.

Even in the moral quicksand of Sodom and Gomorrah, God saw that there was good. God remembered the righteousness of Abraham, and for the sake of God's relationship with Abraham, God saved Abraham's nephew and his family. The angels of God warned Lot to leave the area. This family was spared. God redeemed the good out of the evil. God, in the final analysis, does not destroy the good with the bad. God did not allow God's anger to destroy everything in its path.

This is why we are required to say a blessing at the place of Sodom and Gomorrah. The memory as framed by the benediction emphasizes the preservation of that which is good, not the destruction of evil.

It is crucial not to destroy the legacy of your marriage, for there was much that was good in it. Much of your personal history is bound up in it. To destroy everything that once existed is to destroy much of your own life. The anger of divorce can be a self-destructive force if we don't understand it and allow it to burn out of control.

And herein lies the lesson of this digression: we must learn to bless the anger as the way to control it. We must not let the anger obscure the good, and we must learn to see the good in the anger, in the function it serves in the healing process.

WHY IS ANGER NECESSARY?

For some, particularly for those who did not initiate the divorce, the divorce constitutes a crippling assault on self-image. The partner who is left feels humiliated, shamed, embarrassed. Self-esteem has been shattered; anger helps to maintain equilibrium. There are those for whom anger serves as a shield to greater depression. The partner who initiated the divorce needs to bless the partner's anger, to understand that it serves a higher purpose. As difficult, painful, and uncomfortable as it is to be the brunt of someone's anger, to bless that anger means to accept its psychological value and absorb its sting without reacting personally. To bless that anger means to appreciate that it is necessary for your partner's emotional and spiritual healing from the wound caused by being abandoned.

For others, anger is a necessary stage in grieving the loss of the marriage. None of us can make the transition to a new life without it. None of us can heal from the trauma of divorce without experiencing anger. None of us can grow through the loss without anger. In this respect, anger serves a therapeutic function that is healthy. In this respect, anger is a spiritual gift and needs to be blessed. It serves us to bring us to a higher level of healing.

When we understand that anger is a necessary part of the grieving process during and after the loss of a relationship, when we realize that it is impossible to make the transition to a place of calm and acceptance after a divorce without experiencing anger, and when we can learn to accept anger—our own, our partner's—as a healthy part of the inner life God created within us, as an emotional construct that mirrors God's inner life, then we can embrace anger without letting it control us.

Ways to Deal with Anger without Causing Damage

The key to blessing anger is to express it, to give vent to it, to articulate it without losing control. I offer the following suggestions as rules of thumb, understanding that the process of going through anger is never easy. Following these principles can serve to shepherd both of you through the stage of anger:

- *Acknowledge the source of anger.* Recognize that your anger comes from your hurt, your disappointment, your shame and embarrassment, your sense of loss, your grief. And then recognize that your ex-spouse's anger comes from the same place. Understanding the pain and hurt in our own soul leads to the same understanding—and, we hope, acceptance—of the pain in our ex-spouse's soul. Accepting our own need to lash out helps us tolerate the very same need in the other. If you do this, the compassion you feel for yourself and for your ex-spouse will mitigate the severity of both your anger and your response to anger.
- *Discount what is being said to you.* We know that in fits of anger and rage, we say things we later come to regret. We know that with the rage that accompanies divorce, the barrage of words that hurt is inevitable. It is to be expected that someone who knows us as well as our ex-spouse will know where our vulnerabilities and sensitivities and insecurities are. In fits of anger, those vulnerabilities will be attacked with heavy artillery. If we distance ourselves emotionally from the onslaught of hurtful words, if we realize that they are being said by someone who is feeling hurt and out of control, perhaps they will be less painful and we will not be as hurt by them. Perhaps.

- *Attack the issues, not the people.* There are legitimate issues arising from separation that allow for honest differences of opinion. There are decisions that need to be made in divorce and agreements to be arrived at. But none of us really wants to be talking about divorce, and none of us really wants to make these difficult, heart-wrenching decisions, and none of us wants to agree to loss and deprivation. It is always easier to attack the other and call the other names than to negotiate division of property and child support and visitation rights. It is easier to hurt and denigrate and damage and tear down another person than it is to solve problems. Try to accept the anger, and redirect the discussion to the issues.
- *Know that to win is to lose.* Oliver and Barbara Rose each wanted to win at all costs, and that is precisely what happened. The cost of their attempts to get the better of the other was total. They lost everything they had spent years building. Each tried to punish the other for real or perceived hurts. It is very easy to allow anger to unleash the urge to strike out at the one who, we believe, has hurt us. Your goal should be to create an environment in which gains are maximized and losses are minimized. Divorce does not have to be a win-lose proposition, but it can be structured in a way that embraces a win-win model.
- *Engage in constructive disengagement.* To take a page from the political scientist's notebook, often the best way to achieve your goals is to remove yourself from the conflict and to disengage emotionally. Although when you're being screamed at and being insulted it feels like a personal attack, although it feels as if integrity is being maligned and character is being assaulted, try not to take it personally. Detach. Take a deep breath. And then take another one. Step back when the other is

yelling. Remain quiet; do not engage in verbal combat. Allowing the other the space to be angry is a great gift, and it gives you the chance, in the end, to achieve your goals.

Remaining silent does not automatically mean that there is agreement or acquiescence. Remaining silent gives the message that progress will not be achieved when there is yelling, when there are insults, when there is verbal abuse. Discussion of the issues can proceed when the outburst is over.

And then you may hope that your ex-spouse will be silent when it is your turn to yell.

- *Remember that anger is just a stage.* Knowing that the unpleasantness of anger is not forever makes it easier to endure—unless, of course, you choose to hold on to it for years to satisfy some negative psychological need. During the worst of it, when it seems unbearable, know that the anger stage is almost over. You will survive this. You will both survive this. You are on the road to acceptance and healing.

So, what do you do with all this anger? First you understand it. Then you embrace it. And then you bless it.

Feel your anger. Give vent to it in nondestructive ways, and then move on. Important work lies ahead of you.

5

The Most Painful Question: How Do We Tell the Kids?

There are many different loves in life…

I heard these words in my head for what seemed like the seven thousandth time. I had rehearsed my speech, over and over again, in dreaded anticipation of what Esther and I were about to do. The time had come for us to tell our three children of our decision to separate. Our opening statement had to be just right, for this was to be a life-transforming experience. What we said, how we said it, where we said it, they would remember forever. This was how we were going to define the meaning of our divorce. We did not have the luxury of a retake. The words had to be perfect.

I had memorized what I was going to say. I knew that if I had not scripted my statement the words would have stuck in my throat, which would be contracting while I was trying to stifle a flood of tears. I knew that the emotions of the moment would cripple my thought process. I also knew that if I left the choice of words to chance, to a sudden spasm of prophetic inspiration, the poverty of my language might cause me to say a wrong word that could wound my children deeply. What we were about to tell them was going to change their lives forever. Nothing that we knew to be normal was going to be the same again. We were about to introduce chaos into all our lives.

Esther and I will both remember that conversation with our children as the single most difficult moment of our lives.

It was a moment we had tried to avoid—for years. Years of beginning conversations only to end them prematurely, because to finish them meant to arrive at the obvious conclusion. Years of denial. Years of acting. All with the goal of preserving an intact family, so that our children's lives would not be disrupted, so that our children would not suffer the chaos of a family disintegrating, so that our children would not be scarred.

Alles fur der kinder, my grandmother used to say in Yiddish. Everything for the children. For centuries parents have sacrificed their own needs to provide for their children. Many couples have stayed together "for the sake of the children." In some cases, this is admirable, commendable, even heroic. It is what parents often do. But, as we have seen, it is not always in the children's best interest for parents to remain together if the home life will be full of strife and conflict.

Sometimes, one reason parents have stayed together is because the moment of truth when they face their children with the dreaded news of a separation is too heartbreaking. Sometimes, it is less painful to remain in a bad relationship than to admit to your children that their lives are going to be transformed forever by divorce. Oh, what we had endured, just so that we did not have to face this moment.

The image for Esther of what we were about to do was of pushing our children off the curb and into oncoming traffic. The metaphor was deeply disturbing, yet apt. The natural instinct of parents is to protect their children from pain. Even when it is a necessary pain, even when the pain serves a greater purpose—such as the pain of inoculations, or the pain of ritual circumcision—a part of us resists with great strength. It is counterintuitive to place one's child in harm's way. After years of pulling them back from the edge of danger, after providing a protective barrier large enough to give them the space to grow yet small enough to protect them, to the best of our ability, from harm, we were about to initiate every parent's nightmare. Who could predict just how painful the news of our impending separation would be? Who could predict whether our children would be emotionally damaged beyond repair, whether the sudden upheaval in our family structure would leave them unable to form healthy adult relationships later in life? Who could predict anything about how any of us would handle this?

The anticipation of this discussion was literally dreadful. I kept thinking of the words of the ancient poet who wrote the biblical Song of the Sea: "Terror and dread fell upon them" (Exodus 15:16).

Esther and I were terrified because we knew the statistics about the children of divorce. We were terrified because we had read the stories, had met some of the kids who were psychologically injured by the breakup of their parents' marriage. What would make us think that one or all of our children would not have their grades drop precipitously in school, or become aggressively violent, or become involved in drug and alcohol abuse, or be unable to function in social situations? Why would our family be spared the high cost of divorce?

We were terrified of inflicting irrevocable damage upon the creatures we love most in life.

Reliving My Childhood Trauma

If the image for Esther was a traffic accident, in me it awakened memories that were thirty years old. It brought back memories of a twelve-year-old boy whose life was changed in a single night.

I was that twelve-year-old boy.

Preparing for the meeting with our children was, for me, an agonizing reenactment of the night when my parents told my brother and me that my father was moving out of the house. That was probably the most confusing and heartbreaking night of my life. Now, I felt as if I were living my parents' life, not mine. The anticipation of this discussion had a deafening ring of familiarity to it, as if I were reliving the failure of my parents' marriage, which I had vowed to myself when I married that I would never do. Not ever.

The discussion we were about to have with our children was a replay of the discussion I had had with my parents, only now I was the parent. The child of divorced parents had grown up to be a divorced parent of children.

And I felt like a failure.

My parents called us into the living room, a formality rarely occurring in my childhood. We were not prone to family meetings. Issues were not shared with the children; our opinions were not sought when a decision affecting all of us had to be made. For us to be called into a meeting meant that we were to be told something important, something epic. And probably something bad.

As we took our places the atmosphere was weighted with anxious anticipation of what our parents were going to tell us. We knew this was not going to be good.

My father did the talking. I don't particularly remember my mother's voice from that night. "We have been meeting with Dr. Gladman," my father said, beginning his soliloquy. That alone provided enough information to confirm that what was happening was not good.

Dr. Samuel Gladman was my mother's psychiatrist. Today, that bit of information is quite unremarkable. But this was 1967. Therapy was something of a novelty; not everyone had a personal relationship with a shrink. Therapy was not a routine avenue for personal growth. A stigma was attached to having a therapist. Only those who were crazy had shrinks. My mother, who had been suffering severe anxiety attacks, had been seeing Dr. Gladman for some time. I remember her, on more than one occasion, in the midst of an episode of severe anxiety, breathing heavily into a brown paper bag in an attempt not to faint. On at least one occasion the bag breathing was not successful, and she fainted. My mother was sent to Dr. Gladman because he was going to fix her.

And now, my father had informed us that not only my mother had met with Dr. Gladman. My father had done so as well. They met with him together.

Scary.

My father continued. He told us of his ulcer and of his conversation with his internist, who advised him that something had to be done to relieve the stress in his life or he was going to lose the lining of his stomach. The source of the stress, apparently, was being married to my mother. And then he told us what they had sat us down to tell us. I can still hear the words: "Dr. Gladman suggested we try a trial separation."

I came to learn later that my parents had no intention of ever getting back together. In truth, when I became an adult and was able to see my parents as individuals, in their own autonomy, separated from my childish need for them to be my parents, I wondered how these two people had ever gone on a second date. They could not have been more incompatible, more unsuited for each other. They had been miserable being married to each other for years, and they had stayed together only for the sake of their children. *Alles fur der kinder,* they were taught, and that was the choice they made. But they each needed, for very good reasons, to get out of their marriage.

But, as I later learned, they told us it was a trial separation in order to soften the blow to my brother and me, in order not to make the message a catastrophic loss, a sudden death. They were trying to protect us from trauma by easing us into gradations of acceptance. At the time, they thought this would be the best for us. Who knew?

I remember turning those words, *trial separation,* over and over in my head in the few days that followed that night, while I struggled to make sense of what was happening to me, to my family. *Trial separation.* What did this mean? I asked with all the sophistication of which a twelve-year-old was capable. Had my parents not made a final decision and they were just testing out a new arrangement? Were they simply angry at each other, as they had been so many previous times, and this time, after they calmed down, after my father's stomach healed, they were going to get back together? And what did my father's stomach have to do with a trial separation? And if this trial is like a test, who grades them, and what do they win? Where was my father going? What did this mean?

Really scary.

By not telling us the truth of their desire to live separately forever, my parents inadvertently added to my confusion. The words *trial separation* allowed me to harbor a fantasy that they would reconcile, that this was just a bad dream that would be over some day. I didn't know for sure precisely what the new reality was to which I needed to adjust.

As I remember, the discussion that night did not last long. My father made the announcement, and then it was essentially over. Living arrangements were discussed. My father was moving out. We were to remain with our mother. We would see my father on Sundays.

Meeting adjourned.

After putting us to bed, my father left the house, suitcases in hand, and moved to his new apartment, many miles away. The last thing I remember my father saying to my brother was, "You're the man of the house now."

He was fourteen. You think *I* was scared?

As I began to read about divorce as an adult, I came to learn how the manner in which my parents informed us left much room for improvement. But what did they know? So few of my parents' friends had gone through divorce. Little if anything had been published at the time to help my parents understand all the issues they were facing. There was little if anything to guide them through the experience or to help them guide us. They were left to fend for themselves through the psychological and social minefield of divorce, and they did the best they knew how.

How Should You Tell Your Kids?

Today, bookstore shelves are lined with self-help books written by mental health professionals who work with families going through divorce. Today, we have the fruits of many years of clinical studies on families making the transition through separation, adjustment, and rebuilding. One can find books on navigating through the separation, on parenting children of divorce, on negotiating the division of property, on litigation and court procedures, on starting over, on blending families when one or both parents remarries. Today, thank God, there are many resources available to help us all along the way. I have learned much from these resources.

I have learned most of all that psychological wounds can be minimized by knowing what is going on inside children when they hear their parents tell them that they are separating. It is easier to know what to say when we know what they are hearing and what they are listening for. Here are some ideas that will help to minimize the trauma.

Tell Them Together

It is critical at the initial discussion for parents to tell their children together, even if they can't stand being in the same room together, even if they want to be as far away from each other as possible, even if they prefer to tell them separately. Telling the children together sends the message that this decision was not decided on unilaterally—even if, in fact, it was. The presence of both parents at this meeting lets your children know that this decision was arrived at by mutual consent, at the end of a long process, by two adults who find that divorce is the best option out of all the others they have tried in their attempt to solve the deep-seated problems of their marriage.

The message being delivered is that both parents were committed to the marriage at its beginning, and both parents are committed to the divorce. The marriage was not entered into irrationally; it is not being terminated irrationally.

It is also important that the children not be separated for this discussion, even though children understand divorce differently at different ages, even though what they need to hear varies depending on their age.

A second message that comes with telling the children together, perhaps even more critical than the first, is this: the marriage is ending, but the family is not. A well-founded fear in children is that one or both of the parents are abandoning them. Abandonment issues accompany every loss, whether it is a death of a loved one or a divorce. This leads to the next important issue.

Many children rightly believe that if their parents can fall out of love with each other, they can fall out of love with them as well. Your family structure is changing, but your love for your children, your intention to care for them, and your desire to share their lives are constants. This is the time to reassure your children of your love for them and of what this decision ultimately means for them, for their needs. They will be able to understand the idea that you are now making the transition from a nuclear family to what Constance Ahrons, in her wonderful book *The Good Divorce*, calls a binuclear family. Your children will now have two homes, two centers of their universe. But what remains unchanging is the love of their parents for them.

It is important to convey to the children that even though the marriage didn't last forever, having them and becoming parents was not a mistake. It was, and continues to be, one of the best parts of the marriage. They are a big reason the parents got married: to have them.

Tell Them at the Right Time

When will you tell the kids? Implicit in this question are two considerations. One, when is the right point in the decision-making process for the parents to have the conversation with their children? Two, what is the right timing for the kids to hear the words?

The final stages of a marriage are marked by conflict and argument. It is important that children be protected as much as possible from the details of the issues between their parents. Fighting should take place away from the children—as difficult as that often is—so that children not become overly anxious whenever an argument breaks out. It is imperative that the "D" word not come up until it is absolutely clear that divorce is the only remedy to the issues between the parents. Children should not think that every fight could lead to a divorce. To learn that married people have arguments and that it is possible to resolve disputes is a valuable lesson. But the more they hear the word "divorce," the greater will be their anxiety and the greater their difficulty in resolving it if the marriage should ultimately be terminated.

It once happened to a woman I know that one morning her children woke up to find their father sleeping downstairs in the guest room while their mother slept upstairs. In the morning, the mother's eyes were red and swollen, and the tension in the air was palpable. When her daughter asked her why they had slept apart, the mother blurted out that mommy and daddy were fighting, daddy is moving out, and he wants a divorce.

Her daughter proceeded to throw up on her shoes.

As it turned out, the father did move out, but only for two weeks. He later moved back home, where he remains until this day. The separation was a temporary one and was part of the attempt to sort out the issues between them. A final decision on divorce had not yet been made. To tell the children before the parents were themselves certain caused undue anxiety in the children.

The second consideration has to do with the timing of the conversation. Your children will forever associate their painful feelings of loss and confusion and anger and fear with events surrounding this discussion. It is not wise to have this conversation with them around holidays or significant family events. You don't want them to forever associate the trauma of your divorce with Thanksgiving, or Hanukkah, or their Aunt Jennifer's wedding. The time you choose for this discussion should be neutral, even if that means you and your spouse have to continue to live together for a while after you have agreed to the divorce. Somehow, that added time of living together is less excruciating when you know you are suffering through it for the benefit of your children.

The time of day is also an important consideration. To tell the children early in the morning as they are about to go to school, or you are about to run off to work, or to tell them late at night just before bedtime does not allow for them to process the information. This is not a conversation that will be absorbed in all its implications and ramifications the first time you have it. You need sufficient time for questioning and crying and talking and more crying, and perhaps yelling, and yes, maybe even vomiting. Your older children in particular will want to talk to their friends. You might consider telling them on a day on which you can bring the children to a preplanned therapy session. Your children will be awash with emotions and concerns that are new to them. By devoting more time to them that first day, and setting up formal family meetings to follow up on questions they will have, you will help them absorb the shock of the news and assimilate its implications.

Tell Them in a Safe Setting

Where will your family meeting take place?

I know a couple who took their kids to their children's favorite restaurant to tell them. Clearly, they thought the restaurant would be a safe place. In reality, they chose the restaurant because it prevented their children from making a scene. Being in a public setting prevented the children from honestly expressing their grief, sorrow, anger, and confusion. The parents picked their children's favorite restaurant because they were afraid of their children's reaction. In effect it was safe only for the parents, and the children have carried that memory with them forever.

I was about to gather all of us into our family room, sitting us on the couches. I didn't realize at the time that I was subconsciously playing my father as I relived the experience of my childhood. I wanted a formal meeting because that was how I remembered the format for such a meeting. As much as I resisted being my father, I was being my father.

Esther had a flash of prophetic insight, for which I will always be grateful. "Let's go upstairs, to our bed," she said.

"All of us on the bed?" I asked.

"Yes, as a family."

It was brilliant. It was informal. It was safe. It was familiar. We had bought a king size bed when we began to have children because we wanted our children to be able to climb into bed with us when they were young. We wanted that cozy feeling of security and intimacy and familiarity and fun as our children were growing up.

Now, as we were informing them that our family was splitting up, Esther instinctively understood the message of the family bed. The message we wanted them to have; no matter what, was that we were going to remain a family. It was going to be a different family from the one any of us knew, with different living arrangements and a different configuration. True, there would be many changes in the future. Esther and I were going to separate from each other, but we were not going to separate from the kids. We intended to remain a family, just one that defined itself differently than before.

The setting for the discussion provided this message. Every family has a place of greatest safety and comfort, a place where the message of family is reinforced. It is possible to find that place—a place that can help minimize the pain and anger and confusion and trauma of this conversation.

Find it. Use it.

Choose Your Words Carefully

One thing psychologists agree on is the notion that the more the children know about what is happening, the less will be their anxiety and confusion. The more they understand, the more empowered they are.

But how much do they need to know?

Some psychologists have suggested that even when the reason for the divorce is infidelity, the children should be told the reason. I hardly think so. Parents do not discuss their intimate life with their young children while married. To do so now is entirely inappropriate. The children do not need to know intimate details that should remain between the two parents. Furthermore, young children do not understand the concept of confidentiality. Know that whatever you tell them is going to be repeated. They are children, and they will need to share their feelings with their friends. In the course of telling their friends, they will repeat everything you say along with some things you didn't.

But there are things they need to know. There are things they must be told.

Different Ages; Different Psychological Needs

Studies have taught us that the psychological needs of children going through divorce—what children think and feel and need to hear—will vary depending on their cognitive and physical development. It is true that many of the emotional and psychological issues that I am going to raise are present to some degree in children of all ages, and there is overlap between age brackets. It may be useful, therefore, to read this entire section. Nevertheless, I have divided the discussion of the psychological needs of children according to age groups to facilitate easier use by parents who only want to look for the discussion pertaining to the ages of their own children.

Preschool- and kindergarten-aged children (ages three to five) face a host of concerns, including a pronounced fear of abandonment, a denial of the divorce, self-blame for the divorce, separation anxieties, and very powerful reconciliation fantasies.

It is especially important to reassure children of this age that first, they will not be abandoned, and second, they are not responsible for the divorce. The guilt experienced by a child of this age can be profound. Preschoolers often recite a litany of "if onlys": if only I was a better child; if only I had been less naughty; if only I had been quieter. Some children internalize the divorce as a personal rejection rather than seeing it as a decision directed by the needs of their parents. To alleviate guilt, to lessen a feeling of responsibility, to shore up self-image, this is what I said:

"There is nothing you did to cause this, and there is nothing you could have done to prevent it."

I repeated this phrase three times over the course of our conversation, until one of my children, rolling her eyes, lifted her hands in exasperation, and said, "Okay, enough already! We understand this wasn't because of us!"

They got the message.

And to address the children's reconciliation fantasies, when children nurse the fantasy that parents will get back together, that they will one day wake up from this nightmare and all will return to normal, this is what I said:

"Some couples do get back together after a separation, but most couples don't."

This acknowledges their hope and accepts it as being normal while rooting them in the reality that the separation will probably be permanent. This is a factual statement. It is true that some couples do get back together, and it is also true that most couples don't.

Younger school-aged children (ages six to eight) face many of the same issues as preschoolers, such as self-blame for the divorce as well as fear of abandonment, and they also need to be reassured that someone will be there to read to them at night and come to their soccer games and take them to piano lessons. But at this level of cognitive development, children begin to be vulnerable to loyalty issues and the need to choose sides in the disputes between their parents. The dangers of triangulation are dealt with in greater depth in chapter 9. For now, suffice it to say that one should, at every opportunity, continue to say positive things about the other parent. But a child of this age thinks very concretely and very practically, and what this child—like every child—needs most is reassurance that his or her basic needs of food, shelter, and clothing will be met. Children need to be assured that they will be taken care of, even though there will be times when money will be scarce. This is what I said:

"You may not get everything you want, but you will always have whatever you need."

Older school-aged children (ages nine to twelve), during emerging adolescence, are particularly susceptible to creating an alignment with one parent against the other. This issue becomes more pronounced as time goes on, as we will see in chapter 9, but mention of it now is important as you craft an opening statement to your children. The vulnerability to triangulation that both parents and older children experience can lead to a subconscious attempt to create an ally even in this initial conversation. It is often the parent who initiates the alignment with the child, soliciting an ally in punishing and seeking revenge against the "guilty" parent. The child internalizes the parent's anger and will join in the attack against the other parent. This alignment comes out of the child's pain, guilt, shame, and loneliness; many times it comes with a desire to force reconciliation.

There are no words to be said out loud for this; there is much to be avoided. During this initial conversation, it is critical that parents speak to their children in one voice. Now is not the time to affix blame, to assuage your guilt, but to let your children know it's not their fault, that they are not the ones causing this.

This is not a time to protect your self-image. This is not a time to protect your ego. This is a time to protect your kids. If you can't be a role model for them in marriage, you can at least be a role model for them in divorce.

Adolescence (ages thirteen to eighteen) is marked by complicated and precarious relationships between parents and children. Adolescence is that period of development when a child goes from being a child to being an adult in a very short time. Adolescents vacillate between bursting forth into independence from parents to retreating into complete dependence, between experimenting with adult behaviors to regressing to childish ones, between idealizing parents as powerful and wise to demonizing them as ignorant fools. Divorce introduces uncertainty and fluidity at a time when a child most needs predictability and security in the home environment in order to most successfully do the work of adolescence. The changes brought about by divorce can be unsettling, to say the least. Adolescents often experience heightened feelings of anger and resentment, and they are enormously conflicted by issues of allegiance and loyalty.

Forthrightness about the causes of the divorce, without divulging inappropriate and unnecessary information about the marriage, is critical in helping a teenager cope with the changes. Furthermore, understanding their vulnerabilities to issues of loyalty helps parents resist the temptation to find an ally among their children. Again, what is not said to a teenager is as critical as what is said.

What I Said to My Kids

Learning from the social scientists who have studied families going through similar experiences to our own helped Esther and me craft an opening statement, a statement on which all subsequent discussions of our divorce were founded. I memorized these words, and to the best of my recollection, this is the way I opened our discussion. This, then, is essentially what I told my children on that day full of dread and terror:

There are many different kinds of love in the world. There's the love your mother and father have for you, which is the strongest kind of love—a love that never changes, a love that never ends. Neither one of us knew that kind of love until we had you. Then there's the love we all have for our other family members, for our grandparents and brothers and sisters and aunts and uncles and cousins. And there's the love you have for your friends, the kind of love where your best friend can know your secrets, and you know they won't tell anyone.

And then there's the kind of love of a husband and wife. When we first got married, we had that kind of love. We thought it would last a very long time. But now we love each other like friends, but not like husband and wife. Sometimes, love between grownups changes. But although we have stopped loving each other like husband and wife, we will always love you.

Your mother and I have decided to separate. We believe it is the best thing for us, and the best thing for our family. A final decision is yet to be made. Some couples do get back together after a separation, but most couples don't.

Know that this is between your mother and me. There's nothing you did to cause this, and there's nothing you could have done to prevent it.

We don't yet know all of the details of living arrangements, but we will tell you what we know so far. Things will be changing, and we will all work this out together. But we want to reassure you that even though you might not get everything you want, you will always have whatever you need. You will not ever go hungry, or not have a place to sleep, or not have clothes to wear.

When I had finished, we cried, we hugged, we cried, questions were asked and answered, and then we hugged and cried some more. There was intense sadness. But remarkably, there was also some laughter. The gnashing of the teeth I had anticipated never came. Our children were able to express their grief, their anger, their sadness, their confusion. They were also able to laugh, to comfort one another, to comfort themselves. It was then I realized that they each had a wellspring of strength they could call upon. I realized they were grounded and centered, that they were going to be able to make the transition through the changes ahead, that they were going to be okay. We were all going to be okay. I was never more proud of them than at that moment. It was then I realized that I want to be like them when I grow up.

Making Order Out of the Chaos of Loss

We cannot shield our children from painful experiences. We cannot create a hermetically sealed environment in which they never know illness, never know deprivation, never know disillusionment or rejection or loss. But neither would we want to. Unless our children learn that they can face adversity and can triumph over it, they will not develop fully as human beings. Pain is a part of life, and one of the greatest lessons we can give our children is that they have the resiliency to overcome pain and grow through loss.

To make order out of chaos is a highly religious act. It is what God did in the beginning, when this entire enterprise of life all started. The beginning of the Bible, the second verse in the Torah, tells us that at the beginning of the process of Creation, the universe was *tohu vavohu*, often translated as "null and void." But what *tohu vavohu* really means is "chaos." When God began to create, the universe was in a state of chaos. Each day of Creation brought a little order out of the chaos. Each day's creation was predicated on the creation of the previous day; each day's creation made the advance of the following day possible.

The initial discussion with your children is a first step in creating order out of the chaos that you are about to introduce into their lives. Knowing as much as each is capable of understanding, as much as is age-appropriate, establishes order. But the first discussion with them is not the last; this process, like God's Creation, needs to continue throughout the months and years ahead. But what you are about to do and what you are about to say will lay the foundations of the new universe that is in the process of emerging for you and your children.

All creation is painful. All creation is unpredictable. All creation is terrifying. But at the same time, all creation is Godlike. Creating an environment that helps your children establish order in a time of chaos is a holy act. Telling your children about the impending divorce is introducing chaos; telling them in a way that anticipates their needs and gives them the seeds of creating order out of the chaos is mirroring the Divine.

It is what God did at the beginning of the universe. It is what you do now.

6

The Ritual Question: How Do I *Get* to Closure?

I have just mentioned that one of the tasks of religion is to create order out of chaos. Chaos is the psychological state in which we find ourselves when we face major change, when we make a transition from one stage of life to another, when we suffer loss, when the world as we thought we knew it no longer exists. Order is achieved when we create a formal structure that is repetitive, predictable, meaningful, and accessible. The primary way religion creates such order is through the establishment of rituals, particularly rituals that mark milestones in life and moments of transition.

Ritual helps us to shape, frame, and give structure to internal thoughts and feelings. Ritual gives voice—in symbol, action, and word—to the inner experience of all those who share in the event of a transcendent moment. Ritual is an eloquent and articulate system to deliver meaning. The power of ritual lies in its ability to capture the eternal issues that are reflected in a particular moment. In this way, ritual makes explicit that which is implicit; it makes external that which is internal.

We begin marriage with an elaborate and well-orchestrated ritual that makes concrete the internal experience of the participants in a wedding. For most people getting married, marriage is not simply a legal arrangement. Even for the most unaffiliated, the most uninitiated, the most distant from organized religion, marriage is a deeply religious act. The significance of what this couple is about to do, of what they are doing, is felt by almost everyone present.

The wedding ceremony is one of the clearest examples we have of ritualizing a transcendent moment in life. Spiritual pores are open to the powerful presence of God as two people publicly enter into the special relationship established by marriage. I see it in the eyes of the bride and groom. I see it in the tears of parents and siblings. I see it in the smiles of the invited guests. This is a holy act, a holy moment.

What is being experienced, what is being established, is not simply a legal arrangement between this man and this woman. This is not about sharing community property, although the economics of marriage is not ignored. Understood by all who participate in the moment of marriage is that these two people are continuing the chain of being. The full weight of history can be felt, as these two do what countless generations of couples preceding them have done. These two bring with them the memories and the stories of their ancestors—people who struggled to create families and to establish homes and businesses, who migrated from place to place and sometimes from country to country—a long historical narrative that includes the story of their own lives coming into being. And now, these two people are taking their place in that historical narrative and directing its destiny, complete with the promise of a future full of infinite possibility, with the expectation of creating new life together, with the hope of achieving intimacy and companionship and lifetime partnership.

It is hard not to feel the holiness of that moment. A minority of couples want to stand before a judge when a marriage begins. Most people want to stand before God.

So people turn to our religious institutions at these transcendent moments, to churches and synagogues and mosques, to celebrate and establish this relationship. People turn to clergy to help them perform ancient rituals that have served generation after generation as a way of expressing outwardly what the participants are feeling inwardly. For this is the job of religion and the stuff of religious ritual.

The need for ritual is as basic a human need as the need for food, shelter, companionship.

Judaism, like every religious tradition, has created rituals that surround significant events of transition from one stage of life to another. From birth to coming of age, to marriage, to death, there are defined and recognizable liturgical structures that have guided countless generations of Jews. Rabbinic manuals provide the means for rabbis to conduct the services of rites of passage. Prayer books contain services for ritual circumcisions and baby namings, weddings, and funerals. The customary psalms to be read are prescribed, the blessings are organized, paragraphs of readings are choreographed, order is given to the chaos of emotions. The ritual tells us what to do, how to do it, when to do it.

Divorce is no less a life transition than marriage. But no invitations are sent out to attend the ritual of divorce. No one hires a caterer, a band, a photographer to capture the fleeting moments of this life cycle event for posterity. While all other life cycle events are public, divorce is intensely private.

What is more, for most people going through it, divorce is only about the stuff of our lives, about the division of community property, about alimony and child support. Even child custody and visitations are negotiated as if they were just stuff. Divorce has been allowed to fall solely within the purview of lawyers and courts to hammer out agreements and settlements and schedules and legal responsibilities. The inner lives of the participants, the ultimate meaning of this moment, are often ignored.

Divorce is not about the division of property; it is about the division of lives. And lives are not divided until there is closure, until both partners accept that a part of their lives and their history is dead and their marriage is over. Closure rarely comes with the decree of dissolution issued by the court. Closure comes when all the parties to the marriage are allowed to be present at the divorce. Closure comes when God is allowed to take a seat at the table.

Marriage is entered into with ritual and clergy and houses of worship and with God. But in most divorces, none of these trappings of religion is present. God is conspicuously absent—exiled, as it were, from the shards of shattered dreams.

But the time when people are feeling most alone, the most abandoned, and the most rejected and dejected is precisely the time when God is needed the most. And God can be present, as God should be, when the ritual of divorce is followed properly.

There is a powerful religious ritual for Jewish divorce that is historic, authentic, meaningful, and effective. It is the central mitzvah of divorce. That ritual of divorce is the writing, witnessing, and delivery of the *get,* the Jewish bill of divorcement. The *get,* as will be explained in greater detail, is a legal document that terminates a marriage, just as the *ketubbah,* the Jewish wedding contract, is the legal document that begins a marriage.

The ritual of Jewish divorce, with the delivery of the *get,* choreographs the death of a marriage. It is a ritual of termination, of cutting off, of final separation, leading to a process of closure. The ritual of divorce is no less powerful and no less sacred than a ritual circumcision or a wedding or a funeral. It is this ritual that gives voice to the pain of radical disappointment, the feelings of failure, the moment of separation between the couple, the death of the marriage, and the need for closure. One period of life ends; another is to begin.

Let's look at the ritual.

WHAT IS A *GET*?

Again, we turn to the biblical verse, as we always must. Once again, the Deuteronomist is painfully clear about the process of divorce but just as painfully ambiguous about the inner lives of a husband and a wife who are going through the experience of divorce:

> A man takes a wife and possesses her. She fails to please him because he finds something obnoxious about her, and he writes her a bill of divorcement, hands it to her, and sends her away from his house (Deuteronomy 24:1).

The Torah's description of divorce is sparse in its detail. An uncharacteristic undercurrent of cruelty, even violence, informs its presentation. The biblical verse breathes the air of finality. The husband is in the position of power; he has made up his mind. There is no attempt to reason with the husband. There is no intervention, no counseling, no second chance for this family. There is only business to be attended to, requirements to fulfill, procedures to follow.

She is to be sent away. She must be sent away.

And so he writes her a *sefer kritut*, literally, "the book of cutting off." This is the Hebrew name the Torah uses to label the bill of divorcement. The rabbinic term for the *sefer kritut* is *get*, and it is by this name that it is known.

A *get* is a simple document. The requirements are exact: twelve lines, no more, no less. All the lines must be of the same length, justified on both the right and the left margins. The paper must be longer than it is wide, with margins on all four sides. Simple, precise, potent.

The text of the *get* contains basic information: the Hebrew date. The place. The names of the parties. The legal formula for separation and divorce. The signatures of the two witnesses, as in every recorded legal document.

According to the Torah, the act of divorce with a *get* requires only the presence of the husband, the wife and two witnesses. Nevertheless, the complexity of the details of Jewish divorce has required that divorce be supervised by experts in Jewish divorce law. Today, as has been the case for centuries, Jewish divorce is conducted in the presence of a *bet din*, a court of three rabbis.

The ritual surrounding divorce is deceptively simple. Divorce is effected by the delivery of the *get* from the husband to the wife. The *get* is written. It is then placed by the husband into his wife's hands. A formula of release is recited by the husband. The wife takes four steps away from the husband, indicating her receipt of the *get* with free will and volition.

The ritual is simple, yet so often misunderstood.

One of the members of my congregation, whom I will call Sarah, called me with a question about the *get* while she was in the beginning stages of divorce. Her husband wanted to arrange for an Orthodox *get* immediately. "He told me he wants closure," she said, while fighting back tears.

After we spoke for a few minutes about how even though she didn't want the divorce she had decided not to fight her husband's decision any longer, she asked me the practical question on her mind: "Tell me," she asked, "should I take someone with me to the *bet din*, the religious court?"

"Well, if you want and need emotional support from someone who is close to you, that would be entirely appropriate," I replied.

"No," she said, "Do I need to take someone who is going to advocate for me?"

She didn't know. She didn't know that the rabbinical court in America doesn't have jurisdiction in matters of civil family law, and she was terrified that the rabbis were going to impose a civil settlement. She didn't know that going before the rabbinical court was not about affixing blame for the failure of the marriage, or imposing judgment, or punishing the parties. She didn't understand what the *get* was all about—and who can blame her? Its meaning has been obscured.

The use of a *get* as the religious ritual for the termination of a marriage, as an instrument of achieving psychological closure from a relationship, is hardly ever spoken of, let alone practiced. In its common usage, the *get* is generally known in one of two ways, if not both: as an instrument of marriage, and/or an instrument of extortion.

Getting the Get *Only in Order to Get Married*

For most people, unfortunately, the *get* has become an instrument of marriage rather than an instrument of divorce because the ritual is delayed beyond the point of its effectiveness. Since most divorces are painfully adversarial, the acquisition of a *get* is often postponed. Even in amicable divorces, the number of decisions that need to be made—division of property, custody, spousal and child support—are exhausting, a seemingly endless minefield of potential eruptions. For many, the *get* is just one more area of negotiation that is avoided. Why go there if one doesn't absolutely need to?

But it is not just the needs and the desires of the husband and wife that contribute to this delay of the *get* ritual.

The Orthodox *bet din*, to its credit, will issue a *get* when asked. The Conservative *bet din*, on the other hand, refuses to issue the *get* until after a civil divorce is complete. There are very good religious, psychological, and practical reasons for the Conservative *bet din* to reexamine its policy.

In the first place, some civil divorces can take years until completion. The policy of withholding a *get* during that period is immoral. It is almost inevitable that either one or both of the partners will become romantically involved with someone else between the legal separation and the time the *bet din* is called. There are two possibilities: either they will be sexually active, or they won't. If one or both chooses to be sexually active before the *get*, the rabbinate has contributed to their committing adultery.

On the other hand, if one or both chooses not to be sexually active before the *get* is issued, only because they are still religiously married, the rabbinate is causing them to postpone intimacy at a time when the need to be held is arguably the greatest. Psychologically, their marriage is over. They are, for all intents and purposes, alone. The *bet din* will have compromised their ability to date, to meet someone special, to rebuild their lives. I trust this is not the intention of the rabbis.

Withholding the Get *to Torment*

Because the ritual of divorce as prescribed in the Torah makes the husband the initiator and deliverer of the *get*, undue power is given to the husband in the termination of the marriage. He orders the *get* to be written; he places it in his wife's hand; he recites the formula of divorce. Her part is passive. She merely receives the *get* and walks with it those few steps.

But what happens if the husband refuses to order the *get* to be written? Even if they live apart, even if they are divorced civilly, they remain married to each other according to Jewish law. The only way to terminate a marriage in Jewish law is with the delivery of the *get*. A woman is unable to marry again in a Jewish ceremony unless and until she receives her *get* from her husband, and it is almost impossible to coerce the man to give his wife a *get* if he chooses to be obstinate. In the event that she never receives her *get*, the wife will remain what is called in Hebrew an *agunah*, which means "a deserted wife." In exercising the power to withhold her freedom from his ex-wife, the husband is in a tremendous position to extort her. He can make her acquiesce to claims and conditions, most often financial, that he would otherwise not be entitled to in a court of law. He can torment her, inflicting enormous emotional and psychological pain on her.

This is despicable behavior. And it is not new. It is as old as Jewish divorce.

In the early first century C.E., Rabban Gamliel the Elder enacted religious legislation that ended an abusive practice during divorce. The specifics of the offensive behavior are too technical to go into great detail here, but suffice it to say that an abusive husband found a way to persecute his wife by using provisions of the law to get around the law. A man would order a *get* to be written to his wife, have it delivered by an agent, and then cancel the *get* before it got to her hand. The document delivered to her was worthless because it had been annulled before it reached her, but the wife didn't know that. She thought she was divorced, but in reality she wasn't. The practice was perfectly legal according to the letter of the law, but did violence to the spirit of the law. The language of the Talmud is *letzaorah huh kah m'khavayn:* the husband's intention was to torment his wife.

The behavior of the husband was insidious, and Jewish law could not, and would not, tolerate it. That a particular behavior is permitted by the Torah does not mean it is kosher, and the Rabbis outlawed this one. To use the Torah for cruelty is to undermine the Torah. Rabban Gamliel, in his wisdom and compassion, established a corrective to curb the power of abusive husbands who would use the ritual of divorce to inflict pain or otherwise manipulate their wives.

Rabban Gamliel provided a brilliant remedy: If anyone arranged for a *get* to be written and delivered to his wife, and then annulled the *get* before it reached her without her knowledge, the *bet din* would automatically annul the marriage retroactively. The court, in availing itself of this remedy, subverted the power of the husband to be abusive in this way.

It is to their everlasting shame that part of the contemporary rabbinate acquiesces to, and thereby participates in, the tormenting of Jewish women by men who use the *get* as leverage in a financial settlement. It is beyond comprehension why the contemporary Orthodox rabbinate does not avail itself of the ancient remedy provided by the Talmud. Why they will not retroactively annul a marriage, thus alleviating enormous suffering in the process, defies understanding. Is this not the spirit of the law, if not the letter, as established by the earliest generations of rabbis? The Conservative *bet din* has annulled in the past, and will continue to annul, marriages in cases where the husband refuses to give his wife her *get*. As we understand the law, this is what is required of us.

Most modern Jews have heard these religious divorce horror stories, and Sarah was afraid that she was walking into a world, unknown and unfamiliar to her, in which the *bet din* was going to support her husband to her ultimate disadvantage. She felt vulnerable, powerless, exposed to the manipulations of strangers. Who can blame her when the ritual of divorce is abused, when rabbis do not always protect the woman?

THE RELIGIOUS AND PSYCHOLOGICAL POWER OF THE RITUAL OF THE *GET*

There is yet another reason why the Conservative *bet din* needs to reconsider its policy of waiting until after the civil dissolution before giving the *get,* other than the one spoken of above. That reason is deeply religious. I did not understand this until I experienced it.

It is one thing to study a religious ceremony while in rabbinical school; it is another to officiate at the ceremony as the rabbi; it is yet a third to live through it as a participant.

Esther and I entered the tiny room at the University of Judaism where the local Conservative *bet din* conducted its business. Three of my senior colleagues, long since retired from congregational life, were the officiating rabbis. There was one table in the middle, running down the length of the room, and a second table, tucked away in a corner of the room, on which the *sofer*, the religious scribe, was to write the *get*. The long table separated Esther and me from the three rabbis, who sat on the other side.

We were all uncomfortable, on edge, perhaps even embarrassed. The senior rabbi of the three was one of my early teachers in rabbinical school. I had known him personally and professionally for over twenty years. But there was no time for small talk. There was business to be attended to. Requirements to fulfill. Procedures to follow.

The first order of business was to establish our Hebrew names. It is critical that the names be correct; the slightest mistake in our names invalidates the *get*. Our *get* must be written specifically for us. It cannot be mistaken for another.

The second step is to determine whether we were doing this of our own free will, whether we were being coerced in any way to terminate our marriage.

After all the many discussions Esther and I had had over the years, after all the questions, the accusations, the months of therapy, yes, we were doing this of our own free will.

And then the rabbi asked a question he is required to ask, a question asked of all people coming to the *bet din* for a divorce:

"Is there a chance of reconciliation?"

Silence. Neither Esther nor I spoke. I was waiting for her to respond first. I glanced at her sitting next to me. Her eyes were turned downward, looking at the table, glassy and unfocused. I have no idea where her thoughts were at that moment. I have never asked her.

But we both knew we were at the point of no return. "No," I finally said, "There is no chance of reconciliation."

We were now ready for the third step, which was to prepare the writing materials. The *sofer* gathered into his hands the paper, the ink, and the quill. Reciting the traditional formula, he presented them to me as a gift. I took them into my hands, indicating my acquisition. They were now mine. I was the sole owner of these materials.

I then proceeded to give them back to the *sofer* with instructions to write a *get* to divorce my wife. There could be no ambiguity. I instructed the *sofer* to write the *get*:

Lishmi. In my name.

Lishma. In her name.

Ulesheim gerushin. In the name of effecting a divorce.

The rabbi then told us to go get a cup of coffee for a half-hour while the *get* was being prepared. An air of surreality surrounded us, as if we were having an out-of-body experience.

When we walked back into the room, the air was stuffy and suffocating. The poor circulation in that tiny room was insufficient to handle the body heat of four adults. A smell of death was in the air.

Esther and I stood facing each other as the rabbi handed me the *get*. As I dropped the *get* into Esther's hands, I said those words, those stark and sharp and searing words of cutting off, the formula of divorce:

Harei zeh gitekh. Behold this is your *get*.

V'hitkabli gitekh. And receive your *get*.

U'vo t'hi m'gureshet mimeni mayakhshav. And with it you will be divorced from me from this moment.

V'harei at muteret l'khol eesh. And behold, you are permitted to every man.

With the placement of this document in her hands and by the recitation of these words, something died in me. The death of my relationship. The death of my marriage. The death of my youthful innocence. The transformation of what once was an intact family into something severed, separate, different, redefined, cut off from each other, cut off from the future. The flow of personal history is shattered.

No longer married to each other, yet still with a shared history. The memories of the love of one's youth, with images of meeting, of courtship, of laughter (so much laughter), of testing the limits of the relationship, of the sharing of intimacies, of the clarity of the moment when marriage was obvious, of planning the wedding with all of its stresses and negotiations and challenges and decisions and finally its magic, of walking down the aisle, of the early attempts to build a home and a family and a life together. So many memories, still shared with the one you will no longer share your life with.

It is, considering the inner lives of the participants, the most unusual death we will ever experience. For most, this is *terra incognita*, unfamiliar ground. Nothing in previous experience has prepared us for this transition. Not even those of us who lived through the divorce of our parents, who grew up in homes with a single parent, fully understood what it meant to divorce, because as we grew up we were distant from the complexities of the relationship of our parents. That was our parents' marriage, and our parents' divorce; our task was to navigate between the two of them, to adjust to a new and different family structure. We were the children, after all, whose main goal in life was to get our own needs met. As children we focused on ourselves. We turned inward, concerned primarily that we would be all right, which is normal, natural, healthy.

But when it is your marriage, and your divorce, it is new ground.

That youthful fantasy of how life was going to be is no longer. The reality of life experiences has shattered the hopes and dreams of postadolescent transition to adulthood. The life partner who was by your side in youth will not be the same life partner in old age.

When the folded *get* was handed back to the rabbi, he cut a tear in one of the corners. This ensured that the *get* could not be used for anyone else, but the gesture was also reminiscent of *kriyah*, the ritual tearing of clothing that attends death and burial. At the cemetery, the clothing (or a black satin ribbon attached to the front of the garment) of the mourners is torn or cut, symbolizing the tearing of the heart that one experiences at the death of a loved one. So, too, with a divorce. The *get* is torn in recognition of the death experience of the participants.

We were in mourning.

When the divorce ritual was complete, the three rabbis extended their hands, smiled, and said:

"We wish you happiness."

I cannot imagine anything more inappropriate to have been said at that moment. I understand what they meant: *We know this is painful, but we also know you will heal from this. You will put your lives back together; you will meet someone new; you will fall in love; you will get married again.*

This may very well be true. Many divorced people do meet someone new, eventually. And many divorced people do fall in love, eventually. And many divorced people do get married again, eventually. But at the moment of separation, at the moment when a marriage has come to an end, the wish for happiness is almost unseemly. Our hearts were broken. The last thing I wanted to hear about was my future happiness.

It is also true that when a thirty-five-year-old woman loses a husband, the odds are good that one day she will heal from this terrible loss, that she will meet someone new, that she will fall in love, and remarry. But would anyone think to walk into the house of *shiva*, into a house of mourning in the first week after the burial, and wish this widow happiness?

To do so would be cruel.

Jewish tradition provides a comforting phrase to say to mourners. We have a stock phrase that gives us something to say when words fail us, when we feel inadequate to comfort one whose heart is broken from the pain of death:

May God grant you comfort amongst the mourners of Zion and Jerusalem.

Implied in this phrase—and what we want a mourner to feel more than anything else—is the sense that the mourner is not alone. God, the source of all comfort, is moved by the cry of the mourner, moved to comfort. Although it does not feel like it at the time of the death, the mourner is told that soon, sometime soon, she will feel the embrace of God's comfort, usually through the people who come to comfort, who are God's hands and arms and feet. At this time of chaos, she is not alone.

The inclusion of the mourners of Zion and Jerusalem is, at first blush, a strange thing to say. This phrase makes reference to the destruction of Jerusalem, so far away and so long ago. What does this have to do with the immediacy of this loss? How is this phrase a comfort?

The destruction of the Temple was a national catastrophe. The world was transformed by this destruction; the world was diminished by the loss of this seat of holiness. The entire Jewish people were forced to adjust to a world without the Temple. We are all mourners of Zion and Jerusalem. None of us is alone in this.

So, too, is the loss of a single human being a national catastrophe. We, all of us, including God, hurt for the loss of this person. We, all of us, including God, need to adjust to a world in which this person is no longer. In a subtle way, she is given the message: she is not alone.

And it is a comfort.

But the rabbis of the Conservative *bet din* are accustomed to ministering to people for whom divorce is a past event, who are ready to remarry and need the *get* in order to do so. Usually, by the time someone comes to the *bet din*, the divorce has been finished. It is no longer a live issue. The memories of the separation and divorce may still inflict pain, inspire rage, and open old wounds, but the memories of the separation and divorce are just that: memories. By the time of arrival at the *bet din*, the divorce is not an event still being lived through, only remembered.

So the rabbis of the *bet din* have grown accustomed to saying something that is appropriate for someone who is about to be married: we wish you happiness.

It is a crying shame. An opportunity for a powerful religious ritual, full of the potential for closure and psychological healing and individual transformation, has been lost. Instead, the delivery of the *get* has as much meaning to most of the participants going through it as filling out income tax forms. No one wants to do it, but we do it because we have to—and rarely any sooner than we have to.

The *get* has become rather a nuisance during the preparation for a second marriage, something that is required by the rabbi about to perform the next marriage.

As a result, in most cases the ritual of the writing and delivery of the *get* is religiously vacuous, a perfunctory performance of a procedural requirement, an empty protocol. Its ability to serve as a ceremony of closure has been compromised, even crippled.

The rabbis of our *bet din* didn't seem to understand that we were going through a death experience, that we were killing something that was once precious to us, that we were dying to a large part of our past. At that moment smiles were not appropriate. Comfort was.

Esther and I wanted to do what was real and what was honest: we wanted to cry. What we had never believed could happen, had happened. We were divorced. Our marriage was over. But we couldn't cry in that little classroom. We couldn't give expression to our honest emotions. We just couldn't cry in front of those rabbis.

We left the room. We stood in the long hallway, and I held Esther as she cried. Ironically, it was while we were separating that we had one of the most powerful moments of intimacy of our entire marriage. Not a word passed between us, but each of us understood the pain in each other's soul. We were sad, and we were scared, and we were vulnerable. We cried as we hugged each other. And there was holiness in that hug. In spite of the enormous changes I was about to undergo, and in spite of the anxiety and fear and enormous pain that those changes were causing, I knew instinctively that I was going to be okay. God was present in that hug, helping me to let go of the anger and disappointment that my life was not going to turn out the way I had planned it. God was present in that hug, reassuring me that in spite of what I felt at that moment, I was not alone.

At that moment, I understood Rashi as I never understood him before. I now understood what he meant when he said divorce is a mitzvah. By performing the religious ritual surrounding the *get*, we had allowed God to enter into a painful moment in our lives. We had experienced the holiness of God's presence through the ritual of the writing and delivery of the *get*.

This was, for me—and I would presume for Esther as well—my *Akedah* experience. The love of my youth died on the altar of divorce the moment I handed her the *get* and said the words of the divorce formula. Like Isaac before me, I ascended that altar to die to my past, to let go of the youthful fantasies of what my adult life was going to look like, to bury that part of my identity that no longer defined me, only to emerge from the altar to begin the transition to my new life.

It was one of the most painful experiences of my life, but in the final analysis it was a gift, and it was a blessing. I felt privileged to get to closure.

7

The Awkward Question: What Do You Say?

The problem of what to say about divorce is a serious one. This chapter is divided into two parts: the first directed to people going through divorce and discussing how to phrase the initial conversation informing people about your divorce; the second directed to people who hear the news directly from someone going through a divorce, and need to find the words to respond. Either way, whether you are the teller or the listener, that initial moment of sharing the information about a couple's divorce is both awkward and painful for both sides of the conversation. Few of us ever handle either side of the conversation very well. That is why I bring this short excursus.

What Do You Say If You Are Getting Divorced?

There are two parts to every verbal communication: what is said by the speaker and what is heard by the listener. Often, those can be two different things.

The speaker chooses words that best appropriate and articulate what the speaker thinks and feels. The speaker thinks that the words which are ultimately chosen reflect what the speaker means.

The listener hears the words of the speaker and filters them through a series of prior experiences and psychological assumptions to hear what the listener thinks the speaker means.

When there is dissonance between these two actions—the speaking of the speaker and the listening of the listener—there is a breakdown in communication that leads to misunderstandings. Not only is it important to find the right words to let people know of your divorce, it is also important to know what your listener could be thinking and feeling when you deliver the news that you are getting divorced. This knowledge can help reduce a great deal of pain for both of you.

The person hearing the news of the divorce hears things that are not being said. Hearing the news triggers deep-seated feelings of vulnerability. Everybody understands there is no inoculation from divorce. Divorce can happen to anyone. At one time or another, every couple has thought about divorce, even if that thought is never articulated but is suppressed. Every couple has worried on some level that the next fight will end in a separation. To have divorce approach the ramparts of one's own marriage by seeing it lay siege to a friend's marriage brings up many suppressed fears. Know that the reaction of your listener will be colored by that anxiety.

Hearing the news of the divorce may also inspire a silent jealousy of the new freedoms that are imagined as a part of the new singlehood. All married people fantasize from time to time about what it would be like to be single again. All married people resent from time to time the restrictions imposed by the ideal of marital fidelity. The one who coined the phrase "gay divorcee" was not a divorced person, I am convinced, but a married person who projected a subconscious desire to be sexually free.

And hearing the news shatters a certain part of the world that your friends have come to know and to rely upon. Married couples often restrict their friendships to other married couples. The divorce of one couple upsets the balance, the symmetry of the relationship. There are loyalty issues: who gets custody of whom? Which one of the divorced couple remains the friend? Is there a danger of taking sides? Is the newly single friend now a sexual threat? Is the divorce contagious? Know that the reaction of the listener will be colored by those fears.

There is a limit to how much people can hear in this first conversation. Because of these and other issues, be prepared to be disappointed by the apparent clumsiness of many people you once considered to be close friends, who turn out to be ill equipped to handle your emotional needs at this moment.

You have a need to talk of your pain, and your friend is worried about his or her own. You have a need to talk about your sadness, and your friend is burdened with his or her own. You have a need for reassurance that you are still considered to be a good person, and your friend has not sorted through his or her own preconceptions and judgments about you and your divorce. You have a need to know that your friend will not abandon you, and he or she is worried about the same thing.

How much does the person you are telling need to know? Initially, the answer is "not much." It is a very good idea to avoid sharing intimate details about your relationship with your spouse until you are confident that the discussion will be private and confidential. When news spreads in your community about your divorce, people will talk about it, often with great detail and even greater authority. You will be shocked and amazed by what people report to you other people have said are the reasons for your divorce. Later, when the news of your divorce has become old news, there will be opportunity to discover the friends who will be willing to talk about your inner life and who will support you when that is needed. And there will be plenty of opportunity to discover who won't be.

When I told people about my divorce, I realized quickly that the best thing for me to say was, "Esther and I have decided to separate. We believe it is the best thing for our family. We thank you for all the love and support you can give us now."

Most people responded by saying, "I don't know what to say." It was the most honest response I received, because the truth is that most people don't know what to say—because what to say is a serious problem.

WHAT DO YOU SAY WHEN YOU ARE TOLD THE NEWS?

This is precisely why Jewish tradition has stock phrases to say for most of life's painful moments. If not for stock phrases, most of us would be mute—or worse, say something hurtful because we think we have to say something, anything, to fill the empty space. We are not comfortable with silence.

This is why Jewish tradition gives us what to say when someone is sick. *Refuah sh'leymah.* May you have a complete healing. And there is a blessing one can say to pray for healing. The *mee sh'bayrakh* prayer is a communal prayer said during the times when the Torah is read liturgically in the synagogue. Scores of people present in the synagogue line up to make sure the name of someone they know who is sick is included in this blessing for healing. God may not have sat on the throne and flipped the switch that made this particular person ill, but God created the world with illness in it, and the task of the human is to live within God's world. If God is ultimately the power that brings illness, God is the power that can bring healing.

We have learned over the years how to live in God's world that contains illness. By publicly identifying the one who is sick and praying for healing, the community is informed and inspired to react with kindness and loving support. Visits and phone calls are made to the hospital room. Flowers and cards are sent. Meals are made to help the other family members concentrate on the tasks they need to do.

Visiting someone who is ill taps into an entire network of anxieties, vulnerabilities, and fears that most of us suppress. We feel no lack of discomfort looking at someone in a hospital bed, because we recognize the randomness that accompanies most illness, and we understand that the patient lying in the bed was struck by a power much greater than the patient, a power over which there was no control. And if that power could strike this patient, it can strike any patient. We recognize that it could just as easily have been us lying in the hospital bed, and being in the presence of the one who is ill reminds us that one day, it probably will be. But even though there is a *mélange* of emotions welling up within us, still, most of us are able to override the discomfort they bring and do the right thing. Still, most of us are able to suppress the voice inside that screams at us to run away.

To do the right thing at that moment is to answer to a higher voice. To do the right thing, to bring comfort, to bring healing, to bring companionship, to bring laughter, is to do a holy act. It is a mitzvah. And we know what to say: "May God bring you a speedy and a complete healing."

Death is another of life's painful moments for which the Tradition provides us something to say. Even though the feelings of anxiety and hurt are greater in the presence of death than in illness, even though our instinct to run away is stronger, there is a blessing to be said when one hears the news of a death: *Barukh dayan ha-emet.* Praised is the God of truth. It has become a cliché to say that death is a part of life, but that it is a cliché does not diminish its truth. It is God's decree that there be death. This is the world God created, and the task of the human is to live within God's world. If God is ultimately the power that brings death, God is also the power that can bring comfort. And we know what to say: "May God bring you comfort amongst the mourners of Zion and Jerusalem."

But divorce is unlike illness and death. Divorce is a death that is not God's doing. Even though Esther and I like to believe, we did believe, that when we got married we were each other's *beshert;* that we were each other's preordained intended; that it was not an accident that we met, came together, fell in love, and began a life together, even though we believed that God orchestrated our marriage from God's perch as the Grand Conductor of life, our separation was not an act of God. This was our choice. This was our decision.

This is perhaps one of the reasons Jewish tradition has not invented a stock phrase to say to people going through divorce. What do you say to people who have decided, whether jointly or unilaterally, for better or for worse, to terminate their marriage? What blessing can be said for this decision that is wholly human?

Still, there is a new reality, and we need to learn to live in God's world that contains divorce.

For this particular moment in life, Judaism has been mute and, in many cases, should be. To say the wrong thing can cause more emotional pain than to remain silent.

The problem of what to say is a serious one. Much goes on within the soul of the listener, both positive and negative. There is much sadness, disbelief, hurt, confusion, and anguish as well as empathy, attentiveness, and love. There is so much going on within us that few of us know what to say.

What not to say is an easier discussion. Most of us have a need to say something, to demonstrate concern and compassion and caring. Most of us want to find the magic words to appropriately respond to the news of divorce. But in the absence of a stock phrase, like those provided in instances of illness and death, many of us say the wrong thing. What follows are some of the more common responses I received in the first few weeks after going public about our separation, and my feelings about their lack of effectiveness.

"Have you tried everything?" Nothing I heard contributed more to my feeling of failure than this question, or stimulated more anger. First, it presumes that every marriage is fixable and every divorce is preventable. It suggests that I just haven't looked long and hard enough to find the solution to my problem. It also suggests a lack of competence in determining the course of my life. Whenever I heard this question I politely excused myself and hung up the phone, or walked away.

"I'm sorry to hear about your divorce, but have I got a girl for you." I heard these words two weeks after my separation, and I continue to hear it years later. Most people believe, deep down, that a person cannot be happy while single. The last thing in the world I wanted to hear was the well-meaning attempt to fix my loneliness by being fixed up with someone's divorced friend. Dating after a divorce is a complicated business, and each one of us will sort it out in our own time. When it is time to be fixed up, we will let you know. I promise.

"You can't do this." Oh, really? Watch me.

"Are you sure?" Do you think we are doing this on a whim?

"This is a tragedy." Thank you very much. That made me feel much better.

"The altar weeps." The people who uttered this quote from the Talmud understood it to mean that God was saddened by my divorce to the point of tears. Another last thing I wanted to hear was how God disapproved of my decision, and how God was disappointed in me. I already had enough sadness without having to take on the extra burden of God's sadness. In fact, as I worked through my decision I asked myself repeatedly, what would God think? I don't know for sure, but I believe that God understands why Esther and I made this decision. If God cried, it was out of deep compassion for the pain we were suffering.

Most people expressed sadness, and that was comforting, and that was effective. All but our closest friends expressed shock and disbelief. But many messages were comforting. I will never forget a long voice mail message I received from a friend—a message I will always appreciate. It began with the words "I am calling to give you a hug." As I listened to the message I realized that was what I wanted most: a hug. I didn't want to feel judged. I didn't want to feel pitied. I didn't want to feel abandoned. I simply wanted comfort and human warmth. That verbal hug was great. I didn't feel alone.

Surely we can find a phrase that speaks to the emotional and spiritual needs of someone going through divorce. Surely we can find the words that capture our hope for someone we care about, someone who is riding an emotional roller coaster, someone who feels as if life has imploded and reality has ruptured. Surely we can find a phrase that lets people know God has not abandoned them. Perhaps the simplest and most helpful thing to say is this: "May God give you strength."

To invoke God at a time when someone feels alone, abandoned, vulnerable, defenseless, the subject of gossip, the object of pity, is a great comfort. This is a time in that person's life when the presence of God is most needed. Your words bringing God into the world are a source of holiness.

And there is holiness in wishing someone going through divorce the requisite strength to persevere while negotiating the never-ending series of decisions that need to be made, the strength to adjust to the countless new situations that will arise, the strength to achieve the triumphs and suffer the failures that lie ahead.

Learn to say the words "may God give you strength." Be prepared to give a hug, whether an emotional or a physical one. Know that to listen to your friend does not mean you are taking sides. It means you are listening to your friend. Listen with a nonjudgmental ear. Know that divorce is not a contagious disease, and this doesn't mean it will happen to you. Know that the decision was not arrived at easily and that there was ample justification for it.

Know this, and then invite your friend over for dinner.

8

The Legal Question: To Litigate or to Mediate?

After it has become clear in the therapy sessions that a marriage has ended, and after the agonizing decision to separate has been made, what remains is to legally terminate the marriage. Marriage is a relationship framed by and rooted in law; it must be terminated in law. And whenever there are legal questions to be decided, there is difference of opinion. Whenever there are differences of opinion, there is conflict. Whenever there is conflict, emotions can spiral out of control. This is the stage of a divorce when things can get really ugly.

Decisions need to be made: decisions that will begin to define the new family structure. Four legal issues need to be decided in a divorce: division of property, alimony, child custody and visitation, and child support. Each of these four areas of decision making is full of land mines and time bombs waiting to go off.

How you and your ex-spouse choose to talk to each other about these four issues will determine the shape of the agreement. No matter what you may feel about each other, no matter how painful it is to be in the same room together, these decisions cannot be avoided. These are the choices, and there are only two: to compete against each other adversarially through lawyers, or to work together to discover what is best for everyone in the family with the help of a neutral third party. Either you litigate, or you mediate. We will explore both of these options here.

LAUGHING THROUGH THE PAIN

A few months after Esther and I separated, my son told me a joke:

> A man walked into a toy store to buy a Barbie doll for his daughter. He asked the clerk behind the counter how much they were. The clerk answered, "Malibu Barbie, $19.95. Doctor Barbie, $19.95. Hollywood Barbie, $19.95. Divorced Barbie, $499.95." "What?!! You're kidding!" exploded the father. "Why is Divorced Barbie so much more than the others?" "Because," the clerk explained, "Divorced Barbie comes with Ken's house, Ken's car, Ken's business, Ken's vacation home…"

My first reaction was to laugh with gusto at that joke. It was a deep, guttural, ear-splitting guffaw. Now that I have experienced the divorce process at first hand, I realize that much about this joke is disturbing. The first thing that bothers me is that at the time of telling, my son was only ten years old.

I ask myself why that joke is funny. Why did I laugh, and how does a ten-year-old boy know that it is funny, and what does this joke say about our culture in general and the culture of divorce in particular?

Divorce jokes are a genre of humor unto themselves, and divorce jokes are not limited to the spoken word. In Beverly Hills there is a famous personalized license plate attached to a very expensive luxury car that says:

WAS HIS

In two words, the owner of the car provided enough information for strangers to fill in the salient details of her personal narrative. She is a divorced woman who was awarded this car as part of her divorce settlement. The car is, for her, a concrete symbol of victory, of her successful attempt to extract as much monetary compensation for her separation and divorce as she and her lawyer could obtain. She is, in a very real sense, Divorced Barbie.

There is nothing funny about divorce, yet we laugh at these and other jokes about divorce settlements. Freud wrote in *Wit and Its Relation to the Unconscious* that humor masks an underlying or subconscious hostility or anxiety that cannot be said directly without offending the listener. To this I might add another function of humor: to acknowledge and affirm a pain that is too sensitive, too sad, too unnerving to talk about directly in a social setting. It would be impolite to upset a crowd of people with the narrative of a divorce battle. No one wants to do therapy in the middle of a dinner party. But to make people laugh about it falls within a socially accepted norm that allows the teller to share feelings that are very real and very raw. So we tell jokes. But behind the laughter there lurks an obvious pain.

At the heart of these jokes lies the recognition that the legal process of terminating a marriage is often excruciating, emotionally wrenching, infuriating, stressful, and expensive. Battles are waged on several different levels simultaneously: psychological, emotional, familial, social, legal, and financial. Especially when there are children involved, legally terminating a marriage is like walking through a minefield. It is possible to walk through the field and never step on a mine, but the odds are not in your favor.

Often, legal professionals are able to help mitigate the difficulties inherent in the process. Lawyers, accountants, judges, and clerks can advise and direct the couple through the maze of the legal system and help them come out on the other side relatively unscathed. But just as often—perhaps even more often—the adversarial system of our courts adds to the anguish of divorce, leaving human carnage in its path.

How Will We Survive Apart?

One thing is certain: each of you will have less money after the divorce than before. It is obvious that the resources available to the couple when there was one household will be stretched thinner when there are now two households to maintain. Along with the anxiety produced by the need to make the transition to a new stage of life, which is scary enough on its own; along with the relationship issues of anger and disappointment and hurt and humiliation, which are emotionally consuming and draining on their own; along with the psychological burden of adjusting to a new self-definition, which takes enormous psychic energy, there is an additional emotional burden that comes from facing the impending reduction in your standard of living.

There is the fear of deprivation, of not having enough, of not being able to hold on to the things that surround you and bring you comfort and stability. Sleep is disrupted as you spend night after night lying in bed, tossing and turning, wondering how you can provide for your children, wondering how to increase your income, wondering how you are going to pay your bills. There is enormous confusion about what you want and what you should do. The one night Father Jacob spent wrestling with his nocturnal demon seems like nothing compared with what you are going through.

Why Is Our Stuff So Important?

On one level, many of the issues in divorce can be reduced to dollars and cents. The dispute is largely about stuff: who is going to get what couch, what bed, what car, what photograph. One would think that the dispensation of material things would be easy. It's not at all, because lurking close to the surface of every discussion, a silent partner in every decision, is a subconscious drama.

Because every object, every item, every dollar, represents something beyond itself. Our assets sheet is not just an accounting of our material worth; it is the blueprint of our lives. It is a map of our journey, recording the turns we have taken, the oceans we have crossed, the mountains we have conquered. We worked long and hard to amass this stuff, and what it symbolizes at this stage of life transcends its material value.

For men, generally speaking, the house, the cars, the jewelry are symbols of success. If your role in life is to hunt bear, the number of pelts you have amassed over the years determines your self-worth in many ways. To lose them makes a man feel like an enormous failure and to experience a diminution of social status. It is an assault on self-image and identity. Men despair at the need to start all over again, as if everything they achieved as a young man was a waste. Not only do men lose the marital relationship in a divorce, they lose a large part of their youth as well. This can lead to some despicable behavior, as when a man tries to hide his assets from his children. But when faced with this psychological battle, it is understandable, if not acceptable, that a man would want to hold on to as much as possible.

For women, again speaking generally, the house, the cars, the jewelry are symbols of security and protection. Even in an age in which women can provide themselves with their own stuff, the material things symbolize the protection and stability and security that were part of her goals for marriage in the first place. Particularly for women who are stay-at-home moms, but even for women who are not, the loss of things represents the loss of security, comfort, and predictability. This is very scary. For some women, the settlement can be compensatory for the loss of protection. A woman about to begin her divorce negotiations, in describing her legal strategy, said to me, "The way I see it, if he can't provide the emotional security and protection I want, well, then, fork it over." When faced with this psychological battle, it is understandable, if not acceptable, that a woman would want to hold on to as much as possible.

Litigating Your Way Through

A great deal goes on inside someone going through divorce, and the adversarial nature of divorce litigation can exploit and exacerbate that vulnerability and anxiety and anger. Because most people have never even observed court proceedings from the gallery, let alone participated in a trial, the experience can be overwhelmingly intimidating and even emotionally crippling. Since the proceedings are uncharted territory for most of us, we must necessarily rely on others to lead us through every decision. When control over one's destiny is given up—even for good reasons—insecurities and vulnerabilities increase. When vulnerability increases, the need to win at all costs becomes greater. If the environment in which divorce is decided is combative rather than collaborative, the result will be that lines will be drawn, positions locked into, heels dug into the sand as each side begins combat with the vow to take no prisoners.

Before beginning litigation, one had better be prepared. Let's listen to what Gayle Rosenwald Smith, a lawyer, says in the introduction to her book *What Every Woman Should Know About Divorce and Custody*:

> Our book seeks to empower women. It gives readers the tools to ask intelligent questions of their lawyers and to make decisions about their conduct so they can win in court. After reading this book, you will not be at the mercy of others. You can take charge of your life and your case and not be a victim of what can be a complicated and mysterious court system.

This particular book is written for women. The message of this book is that women are at a distinct disadvantage in divorce proceedings because the average woman is less familiar with legal and financial matters and, if not armed with knowledge and vigilance, will be victimized by the system.

We can imagine the same kind of book written for men. We can imagine a book written by a lawyer that emphasizes a man's fear of living alone, in a strange apartment, without a woman to rely on; fear of becoming a stranger to his children; of being marginalized and made unimportant by limited contact with them in a bad custody arrangement; fear of being impoverished by alimony and child support orders that leave him with precious little—and prepares the man for battle.

When the legal process is fed by fear and powered by anxiety, the potential for a long, drawn-out, expensive, and painful legal battle is increased. And at the end of the day, when the dust settles, we can only wonder who really wins in that process.

How Far Will You Go to Win?

Some people believe that the only way to be protected in a divorce is to be represented by a barracuda lawyer.

The goal of litigation, quite simply, is to win. Litigation involves two adversaries, represented by their advocates, appearing before an impartial judge. One side presents; the other rebuts. One side provides testimony; the other cross-examines. The judge, in an ideal situation, unbiased, interested only in applying the law, rules on the facts of the case with Solomonic wisdom.

Litigation requires everyone to put ultimate power into the hands of a stranger, but the reality is that not every judge is as wise as Solomon. Moreover, even a judge with Solomonic wisdom is not necessarily someone you want, particularly when issues like child custody are being decided. In perhaps the most famous case of child custody ever tried before a judge, the Bible tells the story of two prostitutes, housemates, who each gave birth to sons, three days apart. Soon thereafter, the first mother claimed that the other woman's baby had suffocated to death when his mother rolled over on top of him in the middle of the night. She awoke in the morning and found the dead baby in her bed, but when she examined it closely, she realized it wasn't her son. She claimed that the second woman switched babies while she was asleep, putting the dead baby in her arms while taking the live baby for her own. She wanted the judge to restore custody of her child.

They began to argue in front of the judge, each claiming parentage of the live baby. In a classic example of judicious compromise, the judge ordered a sword to be brought and the baby cut in half, in order to give an equal share of the baby to each mother.

That judge was none other than King Solomon himself. One woman pleaded with the king not to cut the baby but to keep him alive and give him to the other woman. The second woman, in her anger, in her vindictiveness, in her need to be right, preferred that neither one of them get the baby and asked that the baby be divided equally between them. King Solomon understood that the woman who wanted the baby alive—even if it meant living without her baby—clearly was the birth mother; the woman who wanted to cut the baby in two was better suited to be a mother-in-law.

Of course, the order to cut the baby in half was just a test to see who had the greater maternal instincts for this child. King Solomon had no intention of actually dividing a live baby in two. But sometimes, in custody disputes, it seems as if the parents are willing to cut their children in half because they are angry, because they want to hurt each other, because they are prepared to use their children as weapons. And sometimes, in custody disputes, it seems as if judges are willing to cut children in half to be fair and even-handed, to do what is right for the parents.

Who knows better what is in the best interests of their children than the parents? In litigation, a biased, flawed judge—who doesn't know either of the spouses or the children, who doesn't know their values, let alone share them—is going to decide with which parent the children will live, and how often the parents get to see them, and when.

It is possible to arrive at an agreement that is in the best interests of the children while litigating a divorce. But all too often, in an adversarial environment, child custody is used as a bargaining chip or, even worse, as a blunt instrument to wound that place where the other is most vulnerable. Children are often held hostage to negotiating positions, and their welfare is secondary to the need to win.

A lawyer is hired to be an advocate, to protect the interests of his or her client. An advocate needs to nuance the facts in a way that presents the best possible case for his or her client. Each lawyer, therefore, presents a biased narrative of marital history in order to position the client to get the best deal. The side with the better lawyer wins.

I heard a lawyer tell the story that changed her practice and her direction in life. She began her career as a ferocious litigator. She was hired by a divorced woman living in San Diego who wanted to move with her children to Las Vegas. Three different attempts with three different lawyers to change the custody agreement with her ex-husband failed. The woman hired this particular lawyer because of her reputation as a tough litigator. The lawyer argued persuasively that the mother should be allowed to move with her children. The court agreed. She won her case. She was elated to have won a difficult case that three other litigators before her had lost.

In the hallway after the trial, the father approached this lawyer with tears in his eyes. He wanted her to know what she had just done. He told her that he could not afford to make trips to Vegas to see his kids; the ruling of the court had effectively removed these children from contact with their father. The lawyer was so focused on winning her case that she missed the obvious point: she won her case, and the father lost his kids.

So what did she win?

And this is the point: divorce cannot ever be about winning, because even if you win, you lose. If children are involved, one of your children's parents will be unable to provide the security and stability your children need, and you want your children to be secure and stable.

All that having been said, it needs to be understood that few cases actually come before a judge for trial. Only about 5 percent of divorce cases are tried before a judge. The two lawyers usually negotiate a settlement agreement that is in the best interests of each of their clients.

Negotiations are enormously complicated, and different lawyers employ different negotiating techniques. Some lawyers are mild and conciliatory; some are caustic and mercenary. Some lawyers have the tendency to make concessions and placate the other side; some are combative and are prepared to take no prisoners.

My experience is that clients seek the personality of their lawyers that matches their own personalities or best serves their goals. A separated individual who wants to seek revenge, who is so angry as to want to go for the jugular, will find a lawyer who is a barracuda. A separated individual who is wracked with guilt, or who wants a quick and absolute separation, will find a lawyer who is more conciliatory.

But the question needs to be asked: Is the litigious approach what you really want? Is it what God wants?

What Is Mediation, and How Can I Be Helped by It?

I am going to suggest quite strongly that in most cases, mediation be attempted as the first step in resolving the legal issues in divorce. If the goal of litigation is to win, the goal of mediation—also known by its legal name, alternative dispute resolution—is to meet as many of the needs of both parties as is possible. Most negotiations follow the win/lose model: I win at your expense; the more I win, the more you lose. And vice versa. On the other hand, mediation is the voluntary attempt to find a win/win solution to a dispute by identifying the interests of every party. In a divorce mediation the spouses sit together with a mediator and collaborate to find the solutions that are in the best interest of the entire family.

A mediator is not an advocate for either side but a neutral third party trained in the principles of mediation. The Academy of Family Mediators requires a training program for its certified mediators that includes completion of a forty-hour family mediation course, two hours of domestic violence awareness training, and at least a hundred hours of face-to-face family mediation in at least ten different cases. The goal of the mediator is to put on the table the issues that require resolution and to help the parties frame the conversation so that there can be a resolution most agreeable to both sides. Because the outcome of divorce mediation is the production of a legal agreement to be presented to the court, most mediators are lawyers. But mental health professionals and clergy can also be trained mediators who will collaborate with an attorney to produce the legal document.

There are distinct advantages to mediation over litigation.

It's Less Expensive

The cost of litigation is generally three times the cost of mediation because fewer professionals are involved in mediation than in litigation. The fees for both litigators and mediators vary by a wide range. Some charge an hourly fee ranging from as little as $40 to as much as $600; most mediators fall within the range of $200 to $300 per hour. A family's assets should, as much as possible, remain to be divided between the two principals. Too often, divorcing couples deplete much of their resources paying for their lawyers and have less money to divide between them. Would you rather put *your* kids through college, or your lawyer's?

It Doesn't Take As Long

With litigation, the timing of the process is subject to the schedules and caseloads of two lawyers, a small army of specialists, as well as a busy court docket. The process can take months to years to complete. In mediation, on the other hand, the parties involved control the timing. Agreement can be reached quickly—most mediators say that agreement can be reached in three to eight sessions—or the parties can decide to proceed more slowly.

You Have More Control

The litigation option, while initially allowing the participants to feel omnipotent, like warriors marching off to victory, actually removes power and strength from both husband and wife. Litigation puts all the decision-making power into the hands of the judge. Mediation allows for the two people who made the adult decision to get married to decide how they are going to divorce. The court, while ultimately the final arbiter in any divorce resolution, will sign off on the agreement that is reached in mediation provided the agreement remains within the bounds of the law. This means that the individual parties retain the power to decide the issues according to what they determine is in their best interest and in the interests of their children. Maintaining control over one's personal destiny is empowering and can shore up a battered ego. The more control we have over our destiny, the less anguish and anxiety we feel. The less anguish we feel, the less hostility and rage we feel toward our ex-spouse, and the more humanizing the divorce process becomes.

It's More Personalized to Meet Your Needs

A mediated agreement will more closely reflect your desires, your needs, your values, and what you think is best for your family. It will not follow a generic standardized protocol, which is essentially what the court imposes. Mediation is the most effective way of ensuring that the agreement will be satisfactory to both the husband and the wife. In mediation, it is easier to uncover the interests of either party and to find creative solutions that accommodate both.

In an ideal world, each judge will be completely neutral, unbiased, impartial, without prejudice. But how many people do you know who fit that description? It is unreasonable to expect complete neutrality. There are three possibilities: either the judge will be biased toward men, which is likely, or the judge will be biased toward women, which is also likely, or the judge may be completely neutral, which is highly unlikely. That's two out of three against you, and against the best interests of your family.

A good mediator understands that there are different ways to handle different conflicts, including enforcement, avoidance, conciliation, collaboration, and compromise.

All of these modes of handling conflict are appropriate at some times in divorce proceedings, but not at all times. A skilled mediator can help uncover the underlying feelings and desires and interests of both parties, help them understand the nature of the conflict, and guide the husband and wife to an understanding of which mode of conflict resolution is most appropriate. But most of all, the mediator can help the husband and wife collaborate on uncovering their interests and empower them to let go of fighting to get everything they want, and helping them get everything they need.

When Is Mediation Not Warranted?

Admittedly, not every divorcing couple is a candidate for mediation. There should not be mediation in cases where there are severe psychological problems, or in cases where there has been domestic violence: physical or psychological abuse of a spouse or, worse, of children. Even the threat of violence will cause the other to give in just to be safe, and the final deal will not be fair. In cases of abuse, the abused party needs the defense of an attorney to protect rights. There should not be mediation if there is a power struggle, when one side is a bully while the other remains passive to appease the other. There should not be mediation in cases where one of the spouses is overly argumentative and disagreeable because of a need to remain involved and attached to the other, and refuses to compromise. There should not be mediation when both parties are not willing to be open and honest, as when there is not full financial disclosure.

But in most divorces, mediation is the optimum way to reach an agreement.

How Can I Make My Divorce Holy?

It is during the legal stage in the divorce process, perhaps more than at any other point along the way, that divorce paradoxically provides the greatest impediment as well as the greatest opportunity to experience the presence of God. When facing a situation that can potentially bring out the worst in us, to transcend our negative impulses and do the right thing is an act of holiness. It is a moment of being fully human, of giving flight to what Lincoln called the better angels of our nature, a moment of reaching out to God for strength, a moment of bringing Godliness into the world. This is the mitzvah of divorce.

The mitzvah of divorce requires complete honesty. Withholding information is a sin. When the negative impulse directs us to try and hold on to everything we can, full disclosure of assets is a mitzvah. Hiding assets violates the prohibitions against stealing, lying, and bearing false witness.

The mitzvah of divorce requires collaboration to achieve the most benefit for the most people. When the negative impulse drives us to punish, to seek revenge, to hurt and humiliate, to try and get as much as we can, then to give up being attached to what we want and focus on what everybody needs is a mitzvah.

The mitzvah of divorce requires us to ask the question: what does God want me to do at this moment? What would God want me to do that is in the best interests of my children? How would God want me to preserve the legacy of my marriage and not destroy it completely? By what process and with what values should I terminate this marriage? To struggle with the answers to these questions is to struggle with the mitzvah of divorce.

Even the Psalmist Leads Us to Mediate

The author of Psalm 34 asked the question: "Who is the person who loves life, who desires years of good fortune?" The core of this question speaks to the heart of what it means to be human, attempting to reduce to a single phrase the most important characteristics a human being can embody. The Psalmist answered: "Guard your tongue from evil, your lips from deceitful speech. Shun evil and do good, seek peace and pursue it."

According to the Psalmist these are the three core values of life. First, we are to be very careful in how we use speech, which is what distinguishes humans from the other animals and empowers us to imitate God. God has endowed us with the faculty of speech and has given us the freedom and the power to use language to speak truth or to speak lies, to speak words that comfort or words that injure, to speak words that bind souls together or words that shatter hearts. Second, we are to embrace all that is good and just and right in the world, even if it is to our own detriment, even if it goes against our self-interest. Third, we are to expend our energy and resources in the pursuit of peace, even—especially—if we have to go out of our way to achieve it.

All three of these core values are present in the considerations of how to legally terminate a marriage. It is easy to love life and pursue peace when God is in heaven and all is well with the world. The greater test is to demonstrate our love for life in the midst of crisis, when pain and disappointment and anger unleash the full fury of our negative impulses and lead us to behave in ways that undermine the ideal of peace.

The decision to mediate, understood in this light, is a decision to embrace the sacred and the holy. It is a decision to transcend ourselves and reach heavenward—and yes, to encounter God. Even if mediation should ultimately fail, the attempt at mediation is one that must be made. In the final analysis, I believe, this is what God calls us to do.

And at the end of the journey there is the possibility of peace—peace in our households, peace in our families, peace in our souls.

9

The Most Important Question: How Do We Continue to Raise Children Together?

I was thirty years old when our first child, Elisheva, was born. In the months leading up to her birth, Esther and I knew that our lives were going to be profoundly different as a result of her arrival, although we had no idea what that difference would be. No previous experience can prepare anyone for the moment when a child is brought into the world and life begins. No book, no movie, no documentary can capture the mystery and the miracle of childbirth. That two little cells could join together, undergo billions of cell divisions, and produce this little child—emerging from the depths of my wife's body—with ten toes and ten fingers and two eyes and a nose and the most perfectly formed pair of lips I had ever seen, transcended comprehension. I understood the biology of it; what I could not fathom was how this could happen, time and again, so perfectly. And even though we knew that birth happens thousands of times a day, day after day, generation after generation, we acted as if we had invented childbirth, as if we were the first couple to experience birth.

My emotional response to Elisheva's birth was so overwhelming that I cried for two and a half days. Every time I replayed the videotape in my head of the moment of her birth, the tears would flow. The emotions came from the deepest part of me, the place where I hide all my secrets and dreams and fears and joys and hopes—the place where I encounter God. Like every other parent, I felt touched by the hand of God as I watched the miracle of birth, the ineffable sight of my child coming out of my wife.

I could not define the source of those emotions.

Years later, I was watching Bill Moyers conduct one of his famous interviews with the late Joseph Campbell, one of the world's leading experts on religious myths. In the course of the interview, Campbell said, "When a baby is born, the parents become part of the generation of death, and the children become part of the generation of life." I heard that and said, Amen. I understood clearly why it was I couldn't stop crying when Elisheva was born.

Campbell meant that when a child is born, the parent is forced to come face to face with his or her own mortality. When a new generation is born, each generation takes one step closer to that great abyss. Death is an inescapable part of life. Part of my emotional response was that Elisheva's birth made me confront the sobering truth that one day I was going to die, and this child was going to live on after me. One of the ways we try to achieve immortality and transcend the finality of our death is to bring children into the world and teach them our values, give them something of ourselves that will live on after we die.

I knew instinctively at the moment my daughter came into the world that my life was no longer about me. I had a different self-definition, another relationship that defined who I am. Until then I had been a son, brother, husband, friend, rabbi. Now I was an *abba*, a father, a dad. This was my newest, most important role in life, the relationship that superseded all others.

Having children is more than merely heeding the biological urge to reproduce oneself, particularly in an age when childbirth is a choice. The act of bringing a child into the world is when we are most Godlike, a moment when humans participate with God as partners in Creation. Parenting contains a spiritual component that transcends biology. Human reproduction is not just so much plumbing, and it is not something that parents do alone. A higher power is necessary to make this happen at all, and it is that power that breathes the soul into each body. God is the source of the soul; parents, from the time their children are born until the time they move out of the house, are the protectors of those souls. We ignore to our own peril the soul work that must continue in children even through divorce.

Parents are willing to sacrifice a great deal for the welfare of their children. We deny ourselves much in order to provide the best education, the best clothing, the best shelter, the best enrichment activities, the best entertainment—in short, the best of everything our resources can provide. We willingly and lovingly give up precious sleep in the middle of the night when a child has a fever. We willingly and lovingly arrange our busy schedules to incorporate their need to be driven all over the city. We willingly and lovingly deny ourselves things like skiing trips or the latest electronic toy or a new suit if it means our kids can go to camp or get braces. We do this without a second thought.

It's what parents do.

That willingness to sacrifice for our children should not end when the marriage dies. The decision to divorce is often arrived at precisely because the hope is that it will allow for better parenting, allow children to grow up in an environment that is free of tension and argument, allow them the possibility (in the case of remarriage) to see an experience of a healthy, loving relationship as the model of what marriage is. But it is critical to stress that even though we divorce each other, parents never divorce their children. We retain that relationship throughout our lives. Our lives still are—ultimately, eternally—about them. That is a piece of the puzzle that never changes, no matter what the family structure eventually becomes.

K'shmo, kakh hu, "as his name, so is he," goes a famous Hebrew saying. Hebrew names are given to Jewish children with great care by new parents. The custom among Ashkenazim, or Eastern European Jews, is to name a child after a deceased relative, while the custom among Sephardim, or Jews from Spain, North Africa, and the Middle East, is to name a child after a living relative. But there is more to a Hebrew name than the choice of a first name. Each Hebrew name contains the patronym and matronym as an integral part of a child's identity. Each Jewish child given a Hebrew name is recognized as the son or daughter of the mother and father.

For example, my full Hebrew name is *Harav Peretz Hayim ben Yitzhak halevi v'Hayah*. I am who I am in relationship, not in solitude, because for my entire life I will be the son of Ivan, from the tribe of Levi, known in Hebrew as *Yitzhak halevi*, and the son of Alice, known in Hebrew as *Hayah*. My parentage is as integral a part of my identity as my first two names. That will not change, even after my parents have lived their allotted 120 years. I will always be their son, even in divorce, even in death.

Just as our parents are an inseparable part of our own identities, so, too, are we equally bound up in the identities of our children. Even in divorce, even in death.

During a divorce, one of the most important series of decisions we make is how we are going to honor that parental relationship. The mitzvot of parenting, the sacred commandments driving parents to rise above self-interest and to care for their children, take on added urgency during this most difficult of transitions. In each step of the divorce process—from the first decision to separate through the end of the youngest child's adolescence—the commanding voice of God is audible to everyone who chooses to listen. Every decision can be measured against God's standard, which demands: *What's in the best interest of the children?*

In every marriage there are inevitable differences—cultural, religious, political, temperamental, parenting style—between spouses. In healthy marriages, those differences are discussed, explored, shared, reflected upon, and discussed again, until compromise and accommodation are reached and household policies are enacted. Sometimes one partner changes to accommodate the other, sometimes both partners arrive at a different position from the ones they started from, sometimes they agree to disagree. In healthy families, children are able to navigate between those parental differences and derive from their parents, individually and collectively, the wisdom and guidance they need.

In a healthy divorce, the dynamic should not be much different. It is true that each parent is now the sole master of his or her home, and decisions can and will be made in each household that reflect the autonomy and freedom of being single. But when it comes to parenting issues, when it comes to deciding where the children will go to school, or how to maintain a healthy social structure or living arrangements, or how to implement rules of behavior based on the values of the parents, having two homes does not lessen the need for two parents to openly discuss and arrive at consistent policies for their children. In a time of emotional chaos and turmoil, what is in the best interest of the children is to provide as much stability as possible.

What children need most of all, if they are to survive the divorce without major trauma, are two parents who continue to be involved in their lives as supportive, nurturing, accessible, interested, guiding figures. They don't absolutely have to have two parents who live together to have that.

But they absolutely have to have two parents who cooperate and collaborate with each other to make that happen. They absolutely have to have two parents who can put the needs of their children ahead of their own. They absolutely have to have two parents who are capable of subordinating their own desires, at least in the short term, in order to meet the needs of their children.

That is never an easy thing to do, but it is the holy thing to do. It is, I am convinced, what God wants of us.

Rising Above Our Anger, Guilt, and Pain

The first rule of parenting, much as in the Hippocratic oath, is "do no harm." To conduct one's divorce badly is to violate this first rule in the most extreme. Studies have shown that continued animosity between parents causes the greatest damage to children as a consequence of their parents' divorce. If parents are able to transcend their negative impulses and cooperate through the divorce, children will more successfully make the transition through the trauma of the loss. But it takes enormous energy and self-sacrifice for this to happen.

You may have difficult relations with your ex-spouse, you may want to avoid your ex-spouse altogether, but one thing is unavoidable: you have lifetime projects together. As long as there are children, the relationship with your ex-spouse will need to remain collaborative. This is what it means to have a child.

But there are things that get in the way of healthy parenting through a divorce. All too often, parents become so wrapped up in the emotional maelstrom of their divorce and in the *sturm und drang* of their own transition that the kids become lost. It takes a great deal of physical and psychic energy to make that transition from a married couple sharing the same household to two individuals living in two separate households. It is even more difficult to make that break when the two are sharing children. It is even more difficult to focus one's energy on meeting the needs of children when we are so needy ourselves. All too often, children get caught in the crossfire between two warring parents.

Moreover, we know our children will be going through a period of pain, anger, fear, confusion, and inner turmoil. We know that the adjustments they need to make will not be easy. We know that the uncertainty of their future causes them enormous anxiety. We know this.

And we also know that we are responsible for the turmoil our children will have to overcome. They didn't ask to be born, and they didn't ask to be bounced between two houses, and they didn't ask for the opportunity to navigate between two parents. This was a series of decisions we made for them. In deciding to divorce, we know we are causing our children anguish, and that willingness to cause pain is counterintuitive to our parental instincts. Our instincts urge us to protect our children from pain, even when we know—as when they received their vaccinations—that a little pain now to avoid a larger pain later is a good thing. The inevitable result is that we feel guilty. Guilt is a vocal stepchild of divorce, and like a toddler in the midst of a tantrum, guilt commands our attention and demands that we respond.

How Should We Raise the Kids?

The most crucial decision we make—after deciding to divorce in the first place—is deciding what kind of divorced parent we are going to be. We have choices to make, paths to follow, and issues to understand and assimilate in order to be the best possible parents.

It takes an enormous amount of inner strength to do the right thing, but deep down inside each human being, at the core of our souls, is a wellspring of strength that we rarely experience and even more rarely call upon. But it is there, nonetheless. It is the place where we store the love of our children. It is that love—precious, priceless, life affirming—that will give you the strength to be the parent you were created to be, even though you are divorced. It is that love that will cause you to be the best you can be.

But in order for that to happen, in order for us to be able to give flight to the better angels of our nature, there are issues in dealing with our ex-spouses that we need to be aware of. These issues will get in our way if we choose to ignore them.

Why We Should Build Up, Not Diminish, the Other Parent

The best parent we can be requires us to collaborate with our ex-spouse, not compete. To cooperate, not undermine. To support, not belittle. But we so much want to demonstrate to our children that the divorce wasn't our fault, that we are not to blame for their pain, that we were justified in dividing the family, that if they only knew what we know they would have done the same thing. Consequently, some parents never miss a chance to point out to their children the inadequacies of the ex-spouse. Somehow, they believe, their guilt will be less if their children can see how unworthy the other parent is.

Eventually in these cases, belittling the other parent results in adult behavior becoming childish and toxic as the need to "get even" and to punish the other becomes irresistible. Fathers may show up hours late to pick up their children. Mothers may make it difficult for fathers to see or talk to their children. A mother may ridicule her ex-husband in the presence of her children or behind her ex-husband's back. Fathers may do the same. This is done in the presence, and with the forced complicity, of children.

We may think that winning the Parent-of-the-Century competition is good for us. We may feel that our children will love us more if they can see how important and valuable we are in comparison with the other parent. But in the final analysis, if we diminish the other parent in the eyes of that child, we are hurting that child. The child experiences this kind of behavior as a personal attack, because the child knows that his or her soul contains a piece of the maligned parent. Each parent is a part of the child; if one parent diminishes the other in the eyes of the child, the child's own self-image is diminished. This is not a time to compete to show who is the better parent or to convince our children which parent is more loving, more capable, more reliable, more involved. It is not in a child's interest to have a parent who is considered inadequate.

It cannot be said any more simply: the more we diminish our ex-spouse in the eyes of our children, the more difficult the divorce will be for them and the fewer will be their emotional resources to cope with the divorce. The more we build up our ex-spouse in the eyes of our children, the more secure and grounded our children will be and the easier the transition will be through divorce.

STRUGGLING FOR POWER THROUGH TRIANGULATION

In the aftermath of a divorce, it is not uncommon for children to find themselves unwilling participants in a tug-of-war as divorcing parents compete with each other for power, for love, and for approval. Whose values will win out? Who will decide the direction of the family? Who will make the major decisions for the child? Who will be valued as the better parent? Who will gain greater affection from the children? Who decides who wins? When these are the silent questions underlying the interactions between parents, the arbiter of the answers is often a child.

The psychological term for including a third party into a dispute is triangulation. When parents make allies out of their children in the power struggle against each other—a conflict that should remain between the parents—the children experience it as an assault on them. Triangulation occurs when one parent tries to get the children to take sides, or when the child is used as a courier of information regarding a dispute between the parents, or when a parent makes a derogatory comment about the other parent in the presence of the child. It is a reversal of roles to make a child choose loyalties, forcing the child into the role of parent, as if the child's judgment were superior to the adults'. The parents need to remain the grownups, and the children must be allowed to be the children.

The psychic wounds of triangulation never heal. Everyone loses at the game of triangulation—even biblical patriarchs.

It happened in the second generation of the patriarchs of Israel, within the marriage of Isaac and Rebekah—who, as you remember, started out so much in love. The stakes were enormously high. Isaac, blind from old age, aware of his encroaching mortality, wanted to put his house in order. He wanted to formally establish which of his twin sons was going to succeed him as the patriarch. The political culture of patriarchal society followed the law of primogeniture, whereby the firstborn son, by virtue of his birth order, received the birthright. The birthright consisted of two things: the position to head the family, and a double portion of inheritance from one's father, while the brothers received only a single portion.

Esau was just minutes older than Jacob, but they could not have been more dissimilar. Esau was a man of brawn, ruddy, earthy, a hunter, a man of the field. Jacob was delicate, a scholar, a homebody.

But Esau was the first born, and as far as Isaac knew, Esau was to get the birthright. Isaac was unaware that years earlier, during adolescence, Esau had sold his birthright to Jacob for a bowl of lentil stew. Isaac was unaware that Rebekah, while the twins were still *in utero*, had received a divine oracle that the blessing of familial leadership would be granted to Jacob, not Esau:

> And the Lord answered her, "Two nations are in your womb, two separate peoples shall issue from your body; One people shall be mightier than the other, and the older shall serve the younger" (Genesis 26:23).

Isaac instructed Esau to hunt for game to prepare the sacred meal that would accompany the ceremony of the blessing of the birthright:

> And he said, "I am old now, and I do not know how soon I may die. Take your gear, your quiver and bow, and go out into the open and hunt me some game. Then prepare a dish for me such as I like, and bring it to me to eat, so that I may give you my innermost blessing before I die" (Genesis 27:2–4).

But Rebekah preempted the meeting between Isaac and Esau by instructing Jacob to bring two kids from the flock, from which she would prepare her own meal. While Esau was still in the field, Rebekah dressed Jacob in Esau's clothes so that he would smell like Esau, covered Jacob's neck and arms with the skin of a kid so that he would feel like Esau, and sent him in to deceive Isaac and to get the blessing from his blind father.

Which he did, with catastrophic consequences.

The result of Rebekah's deception and manipulation was that her family fell apart. Esau flew into a homicidal rage, vowing to kill Jacob. Jacob was forced to leave home, flee for his life, and live in exile for twenty years, never to see his mother again. Esau was so hurt and angry that he also left home, settling in the territory of Mt. Seir, east of the Jordan River. And why? Because Rebekah, who should have known better than to put her sons in harm's way, who should have been able to speak directly to her husband, who should have shared with him the oracle she had received years earlier, opted instead to make an ally out of one son in order to have more power than her husband. When one feels insecure, it is easier to manipulate than to risk rejection or argument.

There is a part of all of us that resists confrontation with an ex-spouse, that finds it more comfortable to be in league with the children, who we know love us, than to be honest and direct with our ex-spouse, who we know doesn't.

But the price of damaging our children's psyches is too great to pay.

How Do We Decide Where the Kids Will Live?

Finding the way to share and divide the responsibilities for raising the children is an imperative, and this goes to the core of the issues that affect physical custody. Determining the schedule of where and when and with whom the children will spend their time is one thing the law requires parents to negotiate. If parents cannot devise a plan about which they agree, the court will decide for them.

Parents often engage in battle over who has authority in raising the children. One of the areas of greatest tension while coparenting through a divorce—and beyond—concerns which parent is the predominant decision maker in the upbringing of the children. Scores of decisions are made weekly, ranging from what the children are going to wear for school, to how their time will be regulated, to which extracurricular activities they will participate in, to patterns of religious behavior. Practically speaking, many of these decisions are made by the parent with whom a child is living at the time the decision needs to be made. It is not uncommon for ex-spouses to argue and disagree about a plan for physical custody because they are fighting for control over raising their children.

The most important consideration is, what is the best custody arrangement for the child? Each child is unique, with a complex matrix of emotional, psychological, physical, and spiritual needs. What arrangement will cause each child the least amount of anxiety, the least disruption to the routine of his or her life, yet at the same time provide the greatest amount of security and parental contact? Parents must be prepared to sacrifice their own personal needs and wishes if those wishes are not in the best interest of their children.

Many options are available to families as they decide who lives with whom, and when. In earlier days, courts would routinely assign primary physical custody to the mother and grant visitation "rights" to the father. The issue of physical custody is no longer automatically decided by gender, and an agreement that makes sense and suits the best interests of the family can be explored fully and negotiated.

But figuring out what is best for your family takes some doing. It is highly recommended that the discussions take place in the office of a therapist or a mediator, to make sure that the decision ultimately arrived at is workable, is best for your children, and is decided for the right reasons.

Physical custody plans can be organized according to percentages of time spent in each of the two homes. In other words, there can be sole custody, equal time, one-third time in one house and two-thirds time in the other, or one-fourth or even one-fifth time in one house and the rest in another. Some families decide that the children will adjust better by remaining an undivided unit; other families decide that some children will fare better with the father as the primary custodian and other siblings will fare better with the mother as the primary custodian. Some families have children switch homes every few days; others decide to switch every other week; still others switch homes every other month, every few months, or even a year at a time.

The custody decision is based on a multiplicity of factors, including the ages and genders of the children, the location of each household relative to the children's schools and friends, the parents' values, and the like. There are many books on the market that talk about child custody arrangements, including analyses of the benefits and pitfalls of each option to help you think them through. A few of the books are listed in "Suggestions for Further Reading." The important thing to remember is that whatever decision is made does not have to be the final one. Living arrangements are open for evaluation and revision, once experience is gained about how they work for the family.

But it is clear from even this cursory summary of the available custody options that the adjustment will be difficult for children. A few families have opted for what sociologists call birdnesting in order to help children make a slow transition through the changes they will have to navigate. In birdnesting, a temporary arrangement not suitable for every family, the children remain in the family home while the parents alternate between living in the family home with the children and living in a rented apartment. This gives the children time to adjust to living with parents separately while at the same time providing them the stability and security of staying in their bedrooms with all of their familiar things. Birdnesting works only when parents can cooperate on sharing two living spaces rather than establishing their own private spaces.

How Do We Not Damage Our Children by Overcompensating and Overindulging Them?

One way divorced parents compensate for their guilt is to buy their children more than they need, as if having more stuff will make their children love them more and be less angry at them. It also attempts to compensate children for their loss of an intact family and for the discomfort of having to move between residences. But blurring the lines between what children need and what children want, by indulging their desires, does not achieve that goal. What it does accomplish is to devalue the worth of material things in the eyes of children and skew their sense of values.

Another way is to relax the rules and restrictions they might normally have imposed had the marriage remained intact, and allow the children the freedom to do things that are not healthy or appropriate, like bending the times of curfew, selecting an inappropriate category of movie for the children to see, or extending the amount of time spent in diversionary activities. Unfortunately, the result of this indulgence is to increase children's anxiety rather than reduce it.

Children—particularly adolescents—need boundaries that are secure, stable, consistent, predictable, and safe. The job of parenting is to let our children understand limits, and the job of childhood is to test limits. They usually do their job better than we do. If those boundaries move in ways that are unreasonable, arbitrary, and capricious, we will quickly send a message that we as parents are unreliable, and that the world they live in cannot be trusted.

As children test limits they shout, beg, bargain, accuse, and try to push every button of vulnerability to get their parents to bend or break their rules. Remaining firm in their resolve not to change the rules is something parents need to do for the sake of their children's mental health.

HOW CAN OUR LONELINESS AFFECT OUR CHILDREN?

One way some parents deal with postdivorce loneliness is to smother their children with their presence because there is something and someone missing in their lives. After years of being defined as part of a pair, after years of being identified as someone's spouse, after years of social invitations that come for two, finding oneself single once again is one of the most difficult parts of divorce. When so much of one's time and energy was devoted to a spouse—even in a bad marriage, even when there was tension and arguing and the absence of real communication—separation from one's spouse creates a vacuum.

Loneliness fills that vacuum.

There is a line between being involved in our children's lives and spending quality time with them as a parent and as a family unit, and using our children to fill the gaps in our own lives. Children need to develop social lives that are healthy and nurturing. If the goal of parenting is to raise children who are grounded, centered, independent, and able to make sound decisions; who demonstrate character and values; who are kind, good, decent, whole, and healthy, then to keep children from their normal activities and interests because the parent doesn't want to do the marketing alone, or to make them accompany the parent to a social obligation because the parent doesn't have a date—all under the guise of spending quality time together—puts pressure on the child to be an adult before the child is ready to be an adult. The goal of raising healthy children cannot be met if we subconsciously use them as surrogate love companions, having them fill in the emptiness that results from the divorce. They are our children, not our escorts.

Moreover, many people going through the loneliness of divorce turn their children into confidantes and speak openly about matters that should not concern them. To share details about one's marriage or about the frightful specifics of one's economic situation, for example, places undue pressure on children. These are grown-up concerns, and children should be allowed to be children. They are our children, not our friends.

A Quick Word about Dating

There is life after divorce, and the issues surrounding the process of postdivorce dating, second marriages, and blended families can fill an entire book—and they do. There are many good books that deal specifically with these issues, and the titles of some of them can be found in "Suggestions for Further Reading." I want to make one point that fits into the concerns of this chapter, and that is the way postdivorce dating affects children.

It is not uncommon after separation from an unfulfilling and unloving marriage for people to seek warmth and affection and validation from someone new. Some people behave as if they had just been let out of prison, and they seek fulfillment in multiple, short-term relationships. Others fall in love in what seems like a matter of minutes and begin long-term relationships. The average divorced man who remarries does so within the first three years of divorce. The average woman takes much longer, if she even remarries at all. But more often than not, those first relationships after separation are transitional. They are part of the transition from being a married person to being a single person—a time of rediscovery of one's autonomous personality.

To introduce someone new to your children before the relationship is serious is to risk increasing levels of anxiety in the children. There are three issues to consider. First, children—especially adolescents—have difficulty conceiving of their parents as sexual beings. To bring a love object into the family dynamic before the relationship has a chance of being permanent will cause undue distress in children that can be permanent. Second, there is a danger of children becoming attached to someone new in your life and then, if that relationship terminates, going through another process of grieving the loss of a relationship and reliving some of the feelings that attended your divorce. The trauma of going through another loss also risks the danger that they will have difficulty forming healthy attachments to mates when they become adults for fear of losing them. Finally, if your children feel that you are giving more energy and attention to a new relationship than you are to them, they will feel abandoned, ignored, and alone. They will carry anger with them for years, perhaps forever.

Children can know that you are not sitting alone at night and feeling lonely, that you are going out in healthy ways with friends, even romantically. But I strongly advise that they not be brought into that relationship before its time.

How Do We Plan and Celebrate Life-Cycle Events?

One day, while talking on the phone in my office, I suddenly heard a voice from outside my office, shouting and screaming. The voice was coming from the office of the senior rabbi. Our offices share a common wall, and when the rabbinic suite was remodeled we insisted that the wall between us be soundproofed. We are both adamant that the conversations in our offices be private and confidential. But this day I was able to hear a voice through the wall, decidedly female. And angry. The decibel level was high enough to penetrate a soundproof wall. It was the voice of rage, and everyone in the building heard it.

So much for confidentiality.

The woman was enraged by something quite innocent, something even good and noble, that the rabbi had done. But he didn't know, he couldn't possibly have known, that by doing the right thing he was touching a very sensitive and very exposed nerve in this mother.

The story is quite simple. It was time to plan the Bar Mitzvah of her son, which had been on the synagogue calendar for over two years. She had been separated from her husband for four years, but the divorce, which had been very contentious, was still not finalized. The father had scheduled a meeting with the rabbi to discuss the arrangements for the Bar Mitzvah, and in the course of the conversation he included the information that he would be paying for everything. The rabbi, touched by the care and concern of the father, and impressed by the apparently loving involvement of the divorced father, settled the Bar Mitzvah arrangements with him.

When the mother heard of this meeting, she immediately called for a meeting of her own with the rabbi. At this meeting she went, as they say, "postal." I could not make out every word, thank God, but these are some of the things I heard her scream:

"He's paying for it all? He hasn't paid a cent of child support in four years! And now he's going to pay for the Bar Mitzvah?

"I'm the member of the synagogue! I'm the one who pays synagogue dues! He could not care less about religious life! How could you make arrangements with him and not me?

"I was the one who brought him each week to religious school! And I was the one who brought him to his Bar Mitzvah lessons! Where the hell has he been that now he comes to you to plan the Bar Mitzvah?"

I don't imagine there is a single clergyperson of any faith who has not had a similar experience. It is part of the minefield of life-cycle events in divorced families. Innocently, unwittingly, with all the best intentions, my colleague had exploded one of the land mines of divorce.

He suddenly found himself in the middle of a power struggle. It was right that the father participate in every way, especially financially, in his son's Bar Mitzvah. And it was right that the mother, who had primary custody of the son, make the decisions for her son's Bar Mitzvah. The painful part of this experience came about because these two ex-spouses could not collaborate with each other in preparing for the most important ceremony in their son's life. That is why the father preempted the mother and made the appointment with the rabbi first, and for himself alone. By going directly to the rabbi before his ex-wife had the opportunity, the father established that his desires for the Bar Mitzvah would be met and the needs of his ex-wife would be ignored.

Ceremonies that celebrate milestones in life—birth and naming, coming of age, marriage, death—will bring to the surface issues that lie dormant within families, if there are any. Whenever relatives gather to publicly mark the passage of time and experience a ritual of transition from one stage of life to another, family structures have the potential of becoming strained and stressed to the point of bitter conflict. Unresolved hurts surface. Old angers are resurrected. New tensions can explode. Families can go for years living with these feelings buried, whispered to each other in private as part of the recitation of the family narrative. But when thrown together in a synagogue or church or cemetery, families have difficulty ignoring these feelings. Strategies that have worked to suppress those feelings, to keep them in check, no longer work when it comes time to celebrate the life cycle.

And when a divorce is involved, the issues can be incendiary.

I know what that is like. My parents separated eight months before my Bar Mitzvah. Both of my parents were brutalized by their divorce; their separation was full of anger and blame and rage and acrimony and scar-forming interactions. On the day of my Bar Mitzvah, I stood on the *bimah*, the forward stage of the synagogue from which the service is conducted, and looked out at the congregation. On one side of the center aisle sat my father's side of the family; on the other sat my mother's side. The hostility and tension in the room was palpable. At times it felt to me like two armed camps, hurling silent accusations and outrage at each other through their glances across the aisle. All the while, my family looked up at me with expressions of pride and joy mixed with pity and sadness. Ultimately, my Bar Mitzvah felt like the furthest thing from a sacred celebration. I don't remember feeling that God was in the room. There was so much anger in the synagogue that there was not enough room for God.

More bad news was that it was impossible, under the circumstances, to throw the kind of Bar Mitzvah party for me that my brother had had just the year before. To celebrate my brother's Bar Mitzvah, my parents had rented a fancy restaurant overlooking the water in the Oakland, California, marina. A nine-piece band played the latest rock tunes while the adults ate and drank too much and the children ran wild through the restaurant complex. That last part is what I remember most about my brother's party, since I was the primary perpetrator. But there was no way my family was going to throw a party for my Bar Mitzvah in the midst of a divorce war.

The irony is that my family felt the need to compensate me for my loss of a party. So they took the money they would have spent on the party and sent me to Israel for the summer. I spent eight weeks in the summer of my Bar Mitzvah year exploring Jewish history in its original location and discovering the roots of my identity. I hardly feel deprived for the lack of a party. In retrospect, it was one of the best things that ever happened to me. But it didn't feel that way at the time.

It would take another thirteen years until my parents were able to be in the same room with each other. It was on the day of my wedding, and the two of them walked me down the aisle: my father on my right, and my mother on my left. They flanked me because of their relationship to me, not to each other.

I was never more proud of my parents than on that day. They did the right thing. They behaved like grown-ups. Their behavior was one of the primary reasons I felt God's presence at my wedding. They taught me that it is possible to transcend personal animosities for the sake of one's children.

Would that everyone could learn that lesson. Some people never learn.

I know someone who was so angry at his ex-wife that he couldn't be in the same room with her. For years. Any contact they had was through lawyers. His children were forced to take sides—either for him or against him—but never allowed to be neutral. Every conversation was a test of loyalties. He stopped talking to one child whom he perceived to be on the side of the mother. As a result, he was not present for either of his daughter's weddings, nor the *brissen* or naming ceremonies of any of his grandchildren. Years later, he was still absent from his first grandson's Bar Mitzvah. He allowed his hatred for his ex-wife to rob his children of a father and a grandfather at a time when they wanted and needed his presence most, and he denied himself the possibility of experiencing some of life's greatest joys. So who was he really punishing?

WHO GETS CUSTODY OF THE *SHUL*?

It is a sad reality that one of the custody issues in a divorcing family is which spouse gets custody of the synagogue or church membership, while the other suffers not only the loss of the marriage and of the family domicile but also the loss of the synagogue or church community just at a time when community support is most needed. There are reasons for this loss that might be understandable but should be overcome.

According to the 2000 population census, the percentage of the American population that reflects intact families, with mama bear and papa bear and baby bears all living together in the same cottage, hovers around 23 percent. This means that more than three fourths of American households fall within the categories of single, divorced, widowed, or married with no children. Yet, one might conclude from reading the rosters of synagogues that much of America looks like Ozzie and Harriet. The overwhelming majority of synagogue members are nuclear families. Religious institutions are conservative in nature, and change within conservative institutions moves very slowly; the culture of most synagogues and churches is still rooted in the sociology of the 1950s and 1960s.

I cannot figure out whether the synagogues create programs for traditional intact families because this is the profile of who joins congregations, and our mission is to serve the needs of our members, or whether our membership consists overwhelmingly of traditional intact families because that is the profile of families for whom we program. My guess is that the answer is both.

The pattern of affiliation with synagogues in the previous generation was what someone called "dry-cleaning Judaism:" in by nine, out by thirteen. Families joined synagogues when the oldest child turned nine and dropped out when the youngest child turned thirteen. These were the years in a Jewish child's life when formal Jewish education began and ended. The first year of religious school was the beginning; the Bar or Bat Mitzvah was the end. That pattern of affiliation has been altered somewhat in recent years in congregations that have an early childhood center. Now, many parents join a congregation when the oldest child turns two years and nine months and enrollment in nursery school is permitted.

The overwhelming majority of divorced singles in my synagogue—as I am sure in almost every synagogue—are there because they have children to educate, not because the synagogue as an institution meets their spiritual and social needs. Many divorced people drop their synagogue membership.

But the time of going through a divorce is precisely when an individual needs what the synagogue or church can offer more than ever: a supportive community, an island of stability, a place to experience God and to cling to a vision of eternity. And a place to learn that you and your family are not alone, that you are not the first ones to go through this, that others have made the transition to wholeness and healing, that you will be all right.

Two things have to change. The synagogue—in its programming, in the way it defines families, in the way both professional staff and volunteers think and speak about families—needs to be more inclusive of singles and single-parent families. Synagogue programming needs to expand to include concern for the needs of the singles population, to be more welcoming and less stigmatizing to families that have not remained intact. Second, synagogue communities need to find a way to help both parents remain members of the synagogue. It is possible to be supportive of each partner in a divorce without taking sides. The adjustment in the synagogue community is difficult at first, and people are uncomfortable with a new family configuration, but the reward is enormous when a binuclear family is integrated into the community.

A final thought:

A member of my congregation reported to me that every time he looks at his eleven-year-old daughter, she reminds him of his ex-wife. She looks like her, displays many of the same mannerisms and attitudes, and even says many of the same words in the same tone of voice as hers. He behaves badly around her, reacting with the rage he thought was reserved for his ex-wife. He becomes short-tempered, yells, says hurtful things he wishes beyond wishing he could take back. He has noticed that he is spending less time with her because of that.

The person we married, with whom we dreamed of building a life and beginning a family, is the same person we fell out of love with, the same person we now can't stand to be around. However, this is also the person who contributed half the DNA to the people we care about most in life, and the person who loves them as much as we do, and the person who is our lifelong partner in raising our children.

If we can focus our energy on our love for our children, we can access that love to help prevent us from hating our ex-spouse and behaving in a way that is destructive. If we can embrace our love for our children and nurture their growth as individuals, we can learn to love that part of our ex-spouse that is a part of our children. If we love our children, we can learn to support that part of our ex-spouse that feeds their souls. If we truly love our children, we won't behave in such a way as to hurt them.

And we love our children.

EPILOGUE

My odyssey with this book began when David walked into my office with a heavy and turbulent soul. He came with the pain of loss, with the anger of radical disappointment, with the burden of guilt and shame, with an overwhelming sense of failure. Speak to me, Rabbi, he said. Tell me of what use my religious tradition will be for me. Help me make sense of my new reality. Inspire me with the age-old wisdom. Connect me to God when I need God the most, when I feel the most alone. Keep me anchored in a community. Help me solve my crisis.

David is by no means alone. He represents, on one level or another, at one time or another, all of us. His personal crisis at that particular moment was his divorce, an event that people currently experience in greater numbers than ever before. But the questions he asked, the tasks he faced, are experienced by everyone who ever suffers a loss, which is all of us.

The implied challenge that David posed was that if he could not find answers from within his tribal traditions, he would search elsewhere. David, like the rest of his generational cohorts, is a good consumer. He knows what he needs. He knows how and where to go to have his needs met and his questions answered. He began with his rabbi, his religion, but in the event I had failed him, he, like many of his generational cohorts, was prepared to seek elsewhere for the answers and the community that he needed.

This book has been a belated attempt to meet his needs, to share with David and others what I have learned from many sources: my own experience, the many members of my community who have come to me, the shared stories of colleagues, the writings of a host of gifted people, the pages of sacred texts.

And I have also learned a profound lesson from lobsters.

Why did God create lobsters and then forbid us to eat them? Does this make sense? They certainly were not created for their beauty. Lobsters are hideously ugly. Lobsters are so ugly I don't know how they reproduce. But I think I know why they were created. They are here to teach us the process of change.

The lobster grows by developing and shedding a series of protective shells. Each time it outgrows its outer shell, it discards it and grows a new one. The lobster remains vulnerable until a new hard shell grows. Then it grows some more and repeats the process. In the meantime, between losing the old shell and developing the new one, it stays exposed and unsafe. If the lobster could speak, it would say it was in a crisis.

Crisis always involves some form of loss: the loss of health, of a loved one, of a relationship, of employment. And as we go through the experiences of loss, the pain, anguish, fear, sadness, and anxiety make life feel unbearable, as if we are not going to survive it. We feel exposed and vulnerable. We feel like Isaac on the altar. We feel as if we are living through our own *Akedah* experience.

One of my inspirations to write this book was a woman who came to me as I was going through my divorce. Her words were offered to me as a comfort and a source of strength. She said, "When my husband left me, I thought my world had ruptured at every seam. I didn't know how I was going to survive it. My self-image was shattered; my financial life was in turmoil. I felt rejected and abandoned by the man who was supposed to take care of me. I felt unattractive, inadequate, and a failure. I was scared to be alone, angry at him for doing this to me, ashamed, and humiliated. Out of financial necessity I went back to school and completed my M.S.W. degree so that I could earn a decent living to support my kids. I'm now doing the kind of work I had started out to do when I was younger but gave up in order to be a wife and mother. I'm still a mother to my children, but I have great satisfaction being a social worker. My friendships are not strained by my being with a man who, I now see, made me bitter and unpleasant to be around. I laugh more, I have more fun, and I feel that I'm a better parent and a better friend. And my children and I have never been closer. I can now honestly say that my divorce was the best thing that ever happened to me."

Was she advocating divorce? Certainly not. I have no doubt that she preferred never to have tasted the bitter water. But what she told me, for which I will be forever grateful, and what guided me through my divorce, were words of encouragement. I could learn from her that it is possible to transform personal tragedy into something positive—if only I was prepared to do the work.

At the end of the Day of Atonement, a very long day of fasting and praying, the holiest day in the Jewish calendar, there is a liturgical service that is unique. It is called *Neilah*, which means the locking of the gates of heaven; it represents the last, final moments for our prayers of supplication and forgiveness to penetrate the heavens and reach the divine throne. As the daylight wanes, as darkness begins to fall, there is the sense that each of heaven's gates is closing, that opportunities for repentance and forgiveness are slipping away. At the beginning of the *Neilah* service stands a paradoxical prayer: *P'takh lanu sha'ar, b'sha'at neilat ha'sha'ar,* "Open for us a gate at the time of the closing of the gates." On one level, it is a last plea to stop the gates from closing, to plead with God to keep it open beyond closing time.

But there is perhaps another way of understanding this prayer. As one gate is locked and then another and yet another, as despair threatens to overwhelm us, as all appears to be futile and pointless, just then the seeds are planted for new birth. Opportunities for personal growth and attaining wisdom rise like a phoenix out of the ashes. As one door closes, another opens. This is what *Neilah* teaches us, and this is what the story of the binding of Isaac teaches us, the story with which we began.

As we make the transition from one crisis to the next, from one stage of life to the next, the biblical story of the binding of Isaac has much to instruct us, much to comfort us, and much to inspire us.

God knows, the narrator knows, and we know that Isaac is not going to be killed in the *Akedah*. God knows, the narrator knows, and we know that Isaac is going to get up off that altar, that he is going to move from one stage of life to another, that he is going to become a stronger, wiser, more mature adult. We call this story the Binding of Isaac, but we really should call it the *Unbinding* of Isaac, because the moment his hands are untied is the moment of climax of the story. That is when the story gains its full meaning, when Isaac goes through this crisis of faith and emerges on the other side physically bruised and emotionally scarred, but ultimately triumphant and transformed. It is when Isaac comes off the altar that the story works as a metaphor for every life journey, yours and mine.

And how do I know that Isaac is all right? Because many years later, when he alone was the patriarch, Isaac faced his own series of challenges. He was a nomadic shepherd; when he faced drought, and his grazing land dried up, he had the strength to change careers, to become a farmer and prosper, even in time of drought.

And then he had conflicts with his Philistine neighbors in Gerar over ownership of wells that once belonged to Abraham and that now belong to Isaac. Isaac was expelled from Gerar and lost his wells; he left without protest. On the outskirts of Gerar, he dug more wells. Again the Philistines claimed ownership; again Isaac did not protest. Finally, after moving again and after digging a third well, he was left alone in peace.

Why did Isaac not stand up for himself at the first two wells? One might think he was damaged goods because of the *Akedah*. One might think he was emotionally crippled, unable to assert himself, cowering from fear of confrontation because of what his father had done to him. One might think that Isaac was a wimp. That is one way of looking at the story.

I think a better interpretation is the opposite one. Because of the *Akedah,* Isaac learned what is important in life and what isn't important. Because of the *Akedah,* Isaac learned that getting into a fight over wells is just not important. They're only wells. How many does he need? There are plenty for everyone. Relationships with people are more important than material possessions. This is what Isaac learned when he went up on that altar. This is what we call wisdom. This is what we call maturity.

At the *Akedah,* God knew that Isaac was going to be all right, and God knows that you are going to be all right as well. While it may be hard to hear when you are in the middle of a crisis like divorce, and it may be difficult to believe, you are becoming a new person, a more grown-up person, a stronger person, a wiser person. It just seems to be a painful fact of life that suffering and pain and anguish and crisis are the catalysts for growth. But if you learn the lessons this experience teaches, if you do the soul work that is required to make the transition through loss, and if you embrace the holy that surrounds you even in your pain, you will be all right.

If you are in the midst of the life crisis catalyzed by divorce, or if someone you love is going through it, know three things. First, it is natural, it is normal, it is developmental to go through crisis; if not this crisis, then something else. Every adult goes through crisis in one way or another, at one time or another.

Second, even though you feel alone, if you are going through a divorce know that you are not alone. You have an array of potential resources to support you. You have a family, you have a community, you have support groups, you have a host of professionals in mental health and clergy who can provide support and guidance, you have a library of books written on divorce, you have God. This is not something you need to face alone.

And third, know that you, like Isaac, have the strength to make this transition. And you, like Isaac, have the strength to be okay. I have learned—from the biblical story of the *Akedah*, and from stories of the people who have come to me—that it is possible to surmount crisis, to grow through loss, to emerge on the other side a stronger, wiser, more loving adult.

A final biblical story:

The Israelites, after having left Egypt, were encamped by the Red Sea. They looked behind them and saw the dust, heard the thunder of the hooves of Pharaoh's horsemen, and his chariots and his warriors chasing after them, rushing to destroy them without mercy. They had no implements of war with which to stand and fight the most powerful army on the planet. To stand still was to face certain death. They looked in front of them and saw a body of water, unplumbed, unbridgeable, impassable. They had no idea how deep the water was; surely to go forward meant to drown. Behind them, in front of them, was death. Everywhere they turned they faced their mortality.

The biblical narrative describes the reaction of the Israelites to this crisis as if this large group of people had spoken in one voice, with one reaction, with one heart. The text records them as saying to Moses, with bitter sarcasm, "What, there weren't enough graves in Egypt that you had to bring us here to die?"

But the Rabbis of the Talmud knew that it is impossible to get so many people together and only have one opinion. The Rabbis suggested four distinct reactions to crisis and gave voice to those four groups of people.

One group among the Israelites wanted to return to Egypt, to return to the subjugation and humiliation of slavery. Better to be dehumanized, they reasoned, than to be dead. Life in Egypt was far from ideal, but it was life. No cause was worth dying for, even if the cause was directed by God.

Others among the Israelites preferred to die by their own hands. In a foreshadowing of the infamous episode on the Dead Sea fortress called Masada, where the last holdout of Judean rebels against Roman authority in 73 C.E. chose to kill themselves rather than allow themselves to be killed by the Roman soldiers—or worse, to be taken into captivity, into slavery, into prostitution—one group of Israelites on the banks of the Red Sea attempted to persuade their brethren to embrace suicide. They had not been the masters of their lives; let them at least now be the masters of their deaths. They did not want to allow their former Egyptian taskmasters to be able to write the final chapter of their lives. Let us kill ourselves, they argued, as the ultimate act of freedom.

A third group was paralyzed by angst and panic. All they could do was to stand and scream: a deep, primal scream emanating from the depths of their viscera. Their legs were frozen with terror, their hands crippled with fear. Staring into the deep abyss, all they could muster was a futile wail.

Only one group, the fourth, was prepared to journey forth into the unknown, to plunge into the sea of uncertainty. For this group there was no other option but forward. Life in Egypt was unbearable; to return was unthinkable, as was suicide. To remain standing was futile. To stand and scream was pointless. They had screamed enough in their lives. It was time to act, to move, to take control of their lives. They pushed on.

These, then, are the options when you face crisis: to return to an unlivable situation, to sit down where you are and literally or figuratively die, to stand still and scream, or to go forward. Given these four options, is there really a choice?

But even among those who had decided to go forward, there apparently was difficulty in moving. Even when they knew going forward was the right thing to do, still the fear of the unknown seemed to freeze their feet. Only one was not crippled by fear and doubt. A famous legend speaks of Nahshon ben Amminadav, a chieftain of the tribe of Judah, the brother-in-law of Aaron, who was the first to follow Moses' command to go forward into the sea. Boldly, according to the legend, Nahshon took a first step into the water. Nothing happened. He continued into the water up to his knees; still nothing happened. He pushed on. He stepped further into the water up to his waist, then to his chest, then to his chin; still nothing. Not until the water was up to his nose, not until he was close to the point of drowning, did the miracle occur and the waters part.

Where did Nahshon get the strength, the courage, to continue into the water? No doubt he expected that the waters would part upon his initial entry into the Red Sea. Surely he was faced with a crisis of faith as he continued to wade deeper and deeper into the water without the anticipated result. Surely he felt as if the whole enterprise was a failure.

But he persisted. He found the necessary strength, because each and every human being has a wellspring of strength upon which we rarely are called to draw. Each and every human being has the strength to do what we need to do. The strength is there. It is a gift from God.

Every year, Jews gather in homes around the world to ritually retell the story of the Exodus from Egypt. The festival of Passover is the only one of the major Jewish festivals that has a nighttime home ritual and liturgical service. The service is to be conducted while the world outside is engulfed in darkness. The ultimate purpose of the yearly gathering is to tell the Exodus story as outlined by the *Haggadah*, the book of liturgy and narrative written especially for this night.

In the middle of the *Haggadah*, just before the meal is to be eaten, there is a powerful little prayer. The prayer speaks to all of us who have ever been in a personal *mitzrayim*, literally a "narrow place," who have ever felt bound and constrained by life's traumas, who have ever suffered a personal crisis. It certainly speaks to those of us who have gone through the loneliness, the disappointment, and the pain of divorce.

> It is our duty, therefore, to thank and to praise, to glorify and to extol God who performed all these wonders for our ancestors and for us. God took us out from slavery to freedom, from sorrow to joy, from mourning to festivity, from darkness to great light, and from bondage to redemption. Let us, therefore, sing before God a new song.

This, ultimately, is the reason we tell the story of the Exodus each year: to remember what happened to our ancestors and to understand that their story is our story too. They suffered under the burdens of slavery. God redeemed them and brought them to freedom. This is God's plan of history. History and our personal lives move from slavery to freedom, from sorrow to joy, from mourning to festivity, from darkness to light. We are told to say this prayer, year after year, to be reassured that the light of spring always follows the darkest winter.

When it feels as if you are surrounded by darkness and can't see your way clear, when it seems that your burdens are unbearable and you are about to collapse, know that this hardship is not forever. You will get through this, and life will again be full of joy. You will grow through this.

And one day soon, God willing, you will be able to say that this experience was all for the best, that you are a better, more sensitive, more giving, more loving person now than you were before the divorce. You will be able to say that you are more capable of loving, more attentive to the needs of those around you, more independent and self-sufficient, more centered and grounded. When that point is reached, a new song will be sung. At present, the tune is still unknown. The lyrics have yet to be written. But the singer is known, and it is you. You are about to find your own voice.

Divorce is a mitzvah. Each step along the process introduces the opportunity to experience holiness. Each step includes the potential for bringing God's presence into the world. Embrace the sacred. For when you do, God will be with you. God will be with you through your darkest hour as your support, your companion, your guide. And God will be with you as you emerge into the light.

May God bless.

Afterword

Afterwards: New Jewish Divorce Rituals

by Rabbi Laura Geller

"When a man divorces the wife of his youth, even the altar of God sheds tears."
—*Gittin 90b*

As this book describes, God is not the only one to shed tears when there is a divorce. Divorce is not only the end of a marriage, but also the acknowledgment of dreams that didn't come true. It is a death that must be mourned before the individuals can go on to create new dreams.

I am a Reform Jew, a feminist, and a rabbi. Like Rabbi Netter, I had worked over the years with many individuals who were going through divorces. I thought I understood their pain, their shame, their anger, and their grief. I had often seen that civil divorce wasn't sufficient to help people separate emotionally as well as financially and physically. I thought I understood the need for Jewish ritual to help them move through their loss to a place where they could begin again. I thought I understood why divinity needed to be present in a divorce in order to increase the possibility of healing. I thought I understood it all, but it wasn't until my marriage ended after twelve years, two children, and a thousand shattered dreams that I really began to understand.

Rabbi Netter is right when he talks about the power of a *get.* It is important. But a traditional *get* alone is insufficient. It is a patriarchal ritual in which a man "releases" his wife and his wife is "released." Yes, I felt I needed to be released, to be set free from the commitments and the promises I had made to this marriage and to the man I had loved since I was twenty years old. The *get* was a necessary first step on the journey to a new beginning.

But it was not enough. I also needed to find a way to release myself, a new ritual in which I was the actor instead of the one acted upon.

In creating new rituals, it is helpful to model them after an existing ritual. At first I thought about mourning rituals, about saying Kaddish over my marriage, but I realized I was beyond that stage. I was ready to end the mourning. The image that came to mind was returning from an unveiling, lifting the veil from a period of intense mourning, and signaling to the mourner and the community that the mourner was ready to "go forth in peace to life." After a funeral, friends bring food and take care of the mourner. After an unveiling, the mourner's status changes; now she can feed those who took care of her. For me, an important part of this new ritual was thanking my friends for taking care of me during my darkest time.

The evening after my traditional *get,* eleven women friends came together to help me create a new ceremony. It was the fifth night of Hanukkah. We began in darkness, sitting in a circle around the *chanukiah.* Each woman shared a story about a journey from darkness to light, stories that were meant to help me on my journey. We lit the *chanukiah* and sang *Shehichianu:* "Thank you God, for having kept us in life, sustained us, and brought us to this time."

Then I read a new version of a *get,* one that I had written. Like the traditional one, it too had twelve lines. But in this *get,* I was the one releasing myself. My *get* also needed witnesses, so after I read it out loud, we passed it around for all my friends to sign.

We went into the backyard and stood near the trees I had planted at the *brit* ceremonies of my son and daughter. Just as I had planted my son's foreskin and my daughter's umbilical cord, so we planted my *get* under a new tree that my friends had given me as a present. As we buried it, I asked each of my friends to speak out loud everything they hoped I could bury from my marriage and divorce.

We returned to the house where I served these friends the best dinner I could cook. After all the months of them feeding and taking care of me, I was finally ready to give something back. On each setting was a present from me to them, to thank them for the gifts of love that they had given me.

We ended the evening with singing and laughing and some tears.

In the years since my divorce, I have worked with many different people to help them create divorce rituals. They have been most powerful when they followed a traditional *get.* But for some Jews, a *get* is not an option. This is particularly true for gay and lesbian couples. Though their commitments are not recognized by the State as marriages, they ought to be acknowledged by religious communities and sanctified by religious rituals. And when these relationships end, the partners need religious ritual just as heterosexual partners do to help them mourn their loss and move forward into healing.

The challenge in creating new rituals is to be certain that they are powerful. For these new rituals to "work," they need to transform individuals, moving them from one stage to another. For new rituals to feel authentic and Jewish, they must connect with the sacred: sacred time, sacred symbols, and sacred words. Like all Jewish ritual, they must simultaneously look backward toward creation and forward to redemption.

Often the timing of the ritual suggests the structure. A divorce ceremony around Rosh Hashana might reinterpret the tradition of *tashlich,* the custom of throwing bread crumbs on the water, as a way to work through what needs to be let go from a marriage that has ended. Sukkot, with the power of the metaphor of fragility, lends itself to a ritual structured around a meal in the sukkah, surrounded by the warmth of friends and the memories evoked through *uzpizin,* inviting the strength that comes from our ancestors and families. To stop and be grateful for the harvest of the marriage, particularly children, helps move from tears to healing. Tu B'shvat suggests a tree planting; Passover, a *bedikat* and *biur chametz,* the search for and burning of the *chametz* of the marriage that is now over. A *tikkun leil Shavuot,* late night study that opens one to clarity and revelation, creates the opportunity for a ritual based around themes of learning and harvest. Tisha B'Av enables one to focus on the destruction of the temple that was the marriage and the hopefulness that is suggested by the promise of rebuilding.

In each new ritual, one needs to ask questions not only about time, but also about setting and community. Typically the rituals I have facilitated have taken place at home. The setting suggests the possibility of transforming and rededicating the space that was once shared by the partners. In this context, it is powerful to remove the mezuzah that was on their bedroom door, burying the *claf* (scroll) and putting up a new mezuzah. If the person has moved into a new home, this ritual is a moment of *chanukat ha-bayit,* dedicating the home by putting up a mezuzah. The community invited could be both those who have been supportive throughout the tough times and those who need to experience the healing that comes from ritual. But unlike a traditional *get,* the presence of the ex-spouse is not necessary.

When people divorce, it is not only God who sheds tears. Divorce rituals, the traditional and the innovative, teach us that while we also cry, there will come a time when the crying can end. These rituals help us understand that we can begin again, grateful for the blessings that have come from our marriage and ready to learn from its mistakes.

English Translation of the Traditional *Get*

The *get,* the Jewish bill of divorcement, is the document that reverses in Jewish law what was established in Jewish law at the time of the wedding. Just as the marriage was initiated with a document—the *ketubbah*—along with a formula of marriage, so too is marriage terminated with a document and a formula of divorce. The language of the *get* is decidedly male. Since historically it was the man who gave the woman the *ketubbah* and recited the formula of marriage to initiate it, it was the man who gave the *get* and uttered the formula of divorce to dissolve the marriage. The structure of the *get* is legalistic and its language is terse:

On the _______ day of the week, the ________ day of the month of ________, in the year ________ since the creation of the world, according to the calculation we are accustomed to here, in the city of _____________ (which is known also as ________,) (that is located on the river __________ and on the river __________), and situated near sources of water, I, ____________ (also known as __________), son of ____________ (also known as _________________) who today am present in the city

__________ (also known as __________), (that is located on the river __________ and on the river __________), and situated near sources of water, do willingly consent, being under no restraint, to release, set free, and put aside you, my wife, __________ (also known as __________), daughter of __________(also known as __________), daughter of __________, (also known as __________) who today is present in the city __________ (also known as __________), (that is located on the river __________ and on the river __________), and situated near sources of water, who has been my wife from time past until now. I do hereby set free, release, and put you aside, in order that you may have permission and the authority over yourself to go and marry any man you may desire. No person may hinder you from this day onward, and you are permitted to be married to any man. This shall be for you, from me, a bill of dismissal, and a document of freedom, in accordance with the laws of Moses and the people of Israel.

Witness 1 ____________________

Witness 2 ____________________

Suggestions for Further Reading

On Divorce

Ahrons, Constance. *The Good Divorce: Keeping Your Family Together When Your Marriage Comes Apart* (New York: HarperCollins, 1995).

Cherlin, Andrew. *Marriage, Divorce, Remarriage* (Cambridge, Mass.: Harvard University Press, 1992).

Fisher, Bruce. *Rebuilding When Your Relationship Ends* (Manassas Park, Va.: Impact Publishers, 1992).

Gardner, Richard. *The Parents Book About Divorce,* revised edition (New York: Bantam Books, 1991).

Hetherington, E. Mavis, and John Kelly. *For Better or For Worse* (New York: W. W. Norton, 2002).

Lew, Alan. *Looking Back on Divorce and Letting Go*. Lifelights: Help for Wholeness and Healing [pastoral care booklet series] (Woodstock, Vt.: Jewish Lights Publishing, 2000).

Seltzer, Sanford. *When There Is No Other Alternative* (New York: UAHC Press, 2000).

Trafford, Abigail. *Crazy Time* (New York: Harper Perennial, 1992).

Wallerstein, Judith, Julia M. Lewis, and Sandra Blakeslee. *The Unexpected Legacy of Divorce* (New York: Hyperion, 2000).

Wallerstein, Judith, and Joan Kelly. *Surviving the Breakup: How Children and Parents Cope with Divorce* (New York: Basic Books, 1996).

Wallerstein, Judith, and Sandra Blakeslee. *Second Chances: Men, Women and Children a Decade After Divorce* (Boston: Houghton Mifflin, 1996).

Weiss, Robert S. *Marital Separation* (New York: Basic Books, 1975).

On Marriage and Relationships

Bridges, William. *Transitions: Making Sense of Life's Changes* (Cambridge, Mass.: Perseus Press, 1980).

Crohn, Joel, Howard Markman, Susan L. Blumberg, and Janice R. Levine. *Beyond the Chuppah: A Jewish Guide to Happy Marriages* (San Francisco: Jossey-Bass, 2001).

Rubin, Lillian B. *Intimate Strangers: Men and Women Together* (New York: Harper and Row, 1983).

Staheli, Lana. *Triangles: Understanding, Preventing and Surviving an Affair* (New York: HarperCollins, 1997).

Wolpe, David. *Finding a Way to Forgive*. LifeLights: Help for Wholeness and Healing [pastoral care booklet series] (Woodstock, Vt.: Jewish Lights Publishing, 2000).

Viorst, Judith. *Necessary Losses: The Loves, Illusions, Dependencies, and Impossible Expectations That All of Us Have to Give Up in Order to Grow* (New York: Fireside, 1998).

On Parenting Children through Divorce

Blau, Melinda. *Families Apart: Ten Keys to Successful Co-Parenting* (New York: Perigee, 1993).

Buchanan, Christy, Eleanor E. Maccoby, and Sanford M. Dornbusch. *Adolescents After Divorce* (Cambridge, Mass.: Harvard University Press, 1996).

Cummings, E. Mark, and Patrick Davies. *Children and Marital Conflict* (New York: Guilford Press, 1994).

Fuchs-Kreimer, Nancy. *Parenting As a Spiritual Journey: Deepening Ordinary & Extraordinary Events into Sacred Occasions* (Woodstock, Vt.: Jewish Lights Publishing, 1996).

Hass, Aaron. *The Gift of Fatherhood* (New York: Fireside, 1994).

Kalter, Neil. *Growing Up With Divorce* (New York: Fawcett Columbine, 1990).

Ricci, Isolina. *Mom's House, Dad's House* (New York: Fireside, 1997).

Shaw, Mary Ann. *Helping Your Child Survive Divorce* (Secaucus, N.J.: Birch Lane Press, 1997).

On Mediation

Fisher, Roger, and Scott Brown. *Getting Together* (New York: Penguin Books, 1988).

Fisher, Roger, and William Ury. *Getting to Yes* (New York: Penguin Books, 1991).

Leonard, Sam. *Mediation: The Book* (Louisville, Ky.: Evanston Publishing, 1994).

Stoner, Katherine. *Using Divorce Mediation* (Berkeley, Calif.: Nolo Press, 1999).

Ury, William. *Getting Past No* (New York: Bantam Books, 1993).

———. *Getting to Peace* (New York: Viking, 1999).

On Grieving & Healing

Brener, Anne. *Mourning and Mitzvah,* 2nd Ed.: *A Guided Journal for Walking the Mourner's Path Through Grief to Healing* (Woodstock, Vt.: Jewish Lights Publishing, 2001).

Breslov Research Institute. *The Empty Chair: Finding Hope and Joy—Timeless Wisdom from a Hasidic Master, Rebbe Nachman of Breslov* (Woodstock, Vt.: Jewish Lights Publishing, 1994).

Breslov Research Institute. *The Gentle Weapon: Prayers for Everyday and Not-So-Everyday Moments—Timeless Wisdom from the Teachings of Rebbe Nachman of Breslov* (Woodstock, Vt.: Jewish Lights Publishing, 1999).

Flam, Nancy. *Yearning for God.* LifeLights: Help for Wholeness and Healing [pastoral care booklet series] (Woodstock, Vt.: Jewish Lights Publishing, 2000).

Schulweis, Harold M. *Bringing Your Sadness to God.* LifeLights: Help for Wholeness and Healing [pastoral care booklet series] (Woodstock, Vt.: Jewish Lights Publishing, 2000).

Schwartz, Dannel I., with Mark Hass. *Finding Joy: A Practical Spiritual Guide to Happiness* (Woodstock, Vt.: Jewish Lights Publishing, 1998).

Wechsler-Azen, Nancy. *Surviving a Crisis or Tragedy.* LifeLights: Help for Wholeness and Healing [pastoral care booklet series] (Woodstock, Vt.: Jewish Lights Publishing, 2000).

Weinberg, Sheila Peltz. *Easing the Burden of Stress.* LifeLights: Help for Wholeness and Healing [pastoral care booklet series] (Woodstock, Vt.: Jewish Lights Publishing, 2001).

About JEWISH LIGHTS Publishing

People of all faiths and backgrounds yearn for books that attract, engage, educate, and spiritually inspire.

Our principal goal is to stimulate thought and help all people learn about who the Jewish People are, where they come from, and what the future can be made to hold. While people of our diverse Jewish heritage are the primary audience, our books speak to people in the Christian world as well and will broaden their understanding of Judaism and the roots of their own faith.

We bring to you authors who are at the forefront of spiritual thought and experience. While each has something different to say, they all say it in a voice that you can hear.

Our books are designed to welcome you and then to engage, stimulate, and inspire. We judge our success not only by whether or not our books are beautiful and commercially successful, but by whether or not they make a difference in your life.

We at Jewish Lights take great care to produce beautiful books that present meaningful spiritual content in a form that reflects the art of making high quality books. Therefore, we want to acknowledge those who contributed to the production of this book.

Stuart M. Matlins, Publisher

PRODUCTION
Tim Holtz, Martha McKinney & Bridgett Taylor

EDITORIAL
Amanda Dupuis, Polly Short Mahoney,
Lauren Seidman & Emily Wichland

COVER DESIGN
Bridgett Taylor

TYPESETTING
Kristin Goble, PerfecType, Nashville, Tennessee

COVER / TEXT PRINTING & BINDING
Lake Book, Melrose Park, Illinois

AVAILABLE FROM BETTER BOOKSTORES.
TRY YOUR BOOKSTORE FIRST.

Spirituality/Jewish Meditation

Aleph-Bet Yoga
Embodying the Hebrew Letters for Physical and Spiritual Well-Being

by *Steven A. Rapp;* Foreword by *Tamar Frankiel* & *Judy Greenfeld;* Preface by *Hart Lazer*

Blends aspects of hatha yoga and the shapes of the Hebrew letters. Connects yoga practice with Jewish spiritual life. Easy-to-follow instructions, b/w photos.
7 x 10, 128 pp, Quality PB, b/w photos, ISBN 1-58023-162-4 **$16.95**

The Rituals & Practices of a Jewish Life
A Handbook for Personal Spiritual Renewal

by *Rabbi Kerry M. Olitzky* and *Rabbi Daniel Judson;* Foreword by *Vanessa L. Ochs;* Illustrated by *Joel Moskowitz*

This easy-to-use handbook explains the why, what, and how of ten specific areas of Jewish ritual and practice: morning and evening blessings, covering the head, blessings throughout the day, daily prayer, tefillin, tallit and *tallit katan,* Torah study, kashrut, *mikvah,* and entering Shabbat.
6 x 9, 272 pp, Quality PB, Illus., 1-58023-169-1 **$18.95**

Discovering Jewish Meditation: *Instruction & Guidance for Learning an Ancient Spiritual Practice* by Nan Fink Gefen 6 x 9, 208 pp, Quality PB, ISBN 1-58023-067-9 **$16.95**

The Handbook of Jewish Meditation Practices: *A Guide for Enriching the Sabbath and Other Days of Your Life* by Rabbi David A. Cooper
6 x 9, 208 pp, Quality PB, ISBN 1-58023-102-0 **$16.95**

Meditation from the Heart of Judaism: *Today's Teachers Share Their Practices, Techniques, and Faith* Ed. by Avram Davis 6 x 9, 256 pp, Quality PB, ISBN 1-58023-049-0 **$16.95**

The Way of Flame: *A Guide to the Forgotten Mystical Tradition of Jewish Meditation* by Avram Davis 4½ x 8, 176 pp, Quality PB, ISBN 1-58023-060-1 **$15.95**

Minding the Temple of the Soul: *Balancing Body, Mind, and Spirit through Traditional Jewish Prayer, Movement, and Meditation* by Tamar Frankiel and Judy Greenfeld
7 x 10, 184 pp, Quality PB, Illus., ISBN 1-879045-64-8 **$16.95**

Entering the Temple of Dreams: *Jewish Prayers, Movements, and Meditations for the End of the Day* by Tamar Frankiel and Judy Greenfeld
7 x 10, 192 pp, Illus., Quality PB, ISBN 1-58023-079-2 **$16.95**

Or phone, fax or mail to: **JEWISH LIGHTS Publishing**
Sunset Farm Offices, Route 4 • P.O. Box 237 • Woodstock, Vermont 05091
Tel: (802) 457-4000 • Fax: (802) 457-4004 • www.jewishlights.com
***Credit card orders* (800) 962-4544** (9AM–5PM ET Monday–Friday)
Generous discounts on quantity orders. SATISFACTION GUARANTEED. Prices subject to change.

Spirituality

My People's Prayer Book: *Traditional Prayers, Modern Commentaries*

Ed. by *Dr. Lawrence A. Hoffman*

Provides a diverse and exciting commentary to the traditional liturgy, helping modern men and women find new wisdom in Jewish prayer, and bring liturgy into their lives. Each book includes Hebrew text, modern translation, and commentaries *from all perspectives* of the Jewish world.

Vol. 1—*The Sh'ma and Its Blessings,* 7 x 10, 168 pp, HC, ISBN 1-879045-79-6 **$23.95**
Vol. 2—*The Amidah,* 7 x 10, 240 pp, HC, ISBN 1-879045-80-X **$23.95**
Vol. 3—*P'sukei D'zimrah* (Morning Psalms), 7 x 10, 240 pp, HC, ISBN 1-879045-81-8 **$24.95**
Vol. 4—*Seder K'riat Hatorah* (The Torah Service), 7 x 10, 264 pp, HC, ISBN 1-879045-82-6 **$23.95**
Vol. 5—*Birkhot Hashachar* (Morning Blessings), 7 x 10, 240 pp, HC, ISBN 1-879045-83-4 **$24.95**

Six Jewish Spiritual Paths: ***A Rationalist Looks at Spirituality***
by Rabbi Rifat Sonsino 6 x 9, 208 pp, HC, ISBN 1-58023-095-4 **$21.95**

Becoming a Congregation of Learners
Learning as a Key to Revitalizing Congregational Life by Isa Aron, Ph.D.; Foreword by Rabbi Lawrence A. Hoffman, Co-Developer, Synagogue 2000
6 x 9, 304 pp, Quality PB, ISBN 1-58023-089-X **$19.95**

Self, Struggle & Change
Family Conflict Stories in Genesis and Their Healing Insights for Our Lives
by Dr. Norman J. Cohen 6 x 9, 224 pp, Quality PB, ISBN 1-879045-66-4 **$16.95**

Voices from Genesis: ***Guiding Us through the Stages of Life***
by Dr. Norman J. Cohen 6 x 9, 192 pp, Quality PB, ISBN 1-58023-118-7 **$16.95**

Ancient Secrets: ***Using the Stories of the Bible to Improve Our Everyday Lives***
by Rabbi Levi Meier, Ph.D. 5½ x 8½, 288 pp, Quality PB, ISBN 1-58023-064-4 **$16.95**

The Business Bible: ***10 New Commandments for Bringing Spirituality & Ethical Values into the Workplace***
by Rabbi Wayne Dosick 5½ x 8½, 208 pp, Quality PB, ISBN 1-58023-101-2 **$14.95**

Being God's Partner: ***How to Find the Hidden Link Between Spirituality and Your Work***
by Rabbi Jeffrey K. Salkin; Intro. by Norman Lear **AWARD WINNER!**
6 x 9, 192 pp, Quality PB, ISBN 1-879045-65-6 **$16.95**; HC, ISBN 1-879045-37-0 **$19.95**

God & the Big Bang
Discovering Harmony Between Science & Spirituality **AWARD WINNER!**
by Daniel C. Matt 6 x 9, 224 pp, Quality PB, ISBN 1-879045-89-3 **$16.95**

Soul Judaism: ***Dancing with God into a New Era***
by Rabbi Wayne Dosick 5½ x 8½, 304 pp, Quality PB, ISBN 1-58023-053-9 **$16.95**

Finding Joy: ***A Practical Spiritual Guide to Happiness*** **AWARD WINNER!**
by Rabbi Dannel I. Schwartz with Mark Hass
6 x 9, 192 pp, Quality PB, ISBN 1-58023-009-1 **$14.95**; HC, ISBN 1-879045-53-2 **$19.95**

The Way Into... Series

A major multi-volume series to be completed over the next several years, ***The Way Into...*** **provides an accessible and usable "guided tour" of the Jewish faith, its people, its history and beliefs—in total, an introduction to Judaism for adults that will enable them to understand and interact with sacred texts.**

Each volume is written by a major modern scholar and teacher, and is organized around an important concept of Judaism.

The Way Into... will enable all readers to achieve a real sense of Jewish cultural literacy through guided study. Available volumes:

The Way Into Torah

by *Dr. Norman J. Cohen*

What is "Torah"? What are the different approaches to studying Torah? What are the different levels of understanding Torah? For whom is study intended? Explores the origins and development of Torah, why it should be studied and how to do it. An easy-to-use, easy-to-understand introduction to an ancient subject.

6 x 9, 176 pp, HC, ISBN 1-58023-028-8 **$21.95**

The Way Into Jewish Prayer

by *Dr. Lawrence A. Hoffman*

Explores the reasons for and the ways of Jewish prayer. Opens the door to 3,000 years of the Jewish way to God by making available all you need to feel at home in Jewish worship. Provides basic definitions of the terms you need to know as well as thoughtful analysis of the depth that lies beneath Jewish prayer.

6 x 9, 224 pp, HC, ISBN 1-58023-027-X **$21.95**

The Way Into Encountering God in Judaism

by *Dr. Neil Gillman*

Explains how Jews have encountered God throughout history—and today—by exploring the many metaphors for God in Jewish tradition. Explores the Jewish tradition's passionate but also conflicting ways of relating to God as Creator, relational partner, and a force in history and nature.

6 x 9, 240 pp, HC, ISBN 1-58023-025-3 **$21.95**

The Way Into Jewish Mystical Tradition

by *Rabbi Lawrence Kushner*

Explains the principles of Jewish mystical thinking, their religious and spiritual significance, and how they relate to our lives. A book that allows us to experience and understand the Jewish mystical approach to our place in the world.

6 x 9, 224 pp, HC, ISBN 1-58023-029-6 **$21.95**

Theology/Philosophy

Love and Terror in the God Encounter
The Theological Legacy of Rabbi Joseph B. Soloveitchik

by *Dr. David Hartman*

Renowned scholar David Hartman explores the sometimes surprising intersection of Soloveitchik's rootedness in halakhic tradition with his genuine responsiveness to modern Western theology. An engaging look at one of the most important Jewish thinkers of the twentieth century.
6 x 9, 240 pp, HC, ISBN 1-58023-112-8 **$25.00**

These Are the Words: *A Vocabulary of Jewish Spiritual Life*

by *Arthur Green*

What are the most essential ideas, concepts and terms that an educated person needs to know about Judaism? From *Adonai* (My Lord) to *zekhut* (merit), this enlightening and entertaining journey through Judaism teaches us the 149 core Hebrew words that constitute the basic vocabulary of Jewish spiritual life. 6 x 9, 304 pp, Quality PB, ISBN 1-58023-107-1 **$18.95**

Broken Tablets: *Restoring the Ten Commandments and Ourselves*

Ed. by *Rabbi Rachel S. Mikva;* Intro. by *Rabbi Lawrence Kushner* AWARD WINNER!

Twelve outstanding spiritual leaders each share profound and personal thoughts about these biblical commands and why they have such a special hold on us.
6 x 9, 192 pp, Quality PB, ISBN 1-58023-158-6 **$16.95**; HC, ISBN 1-58023-066-0 **$21.95**

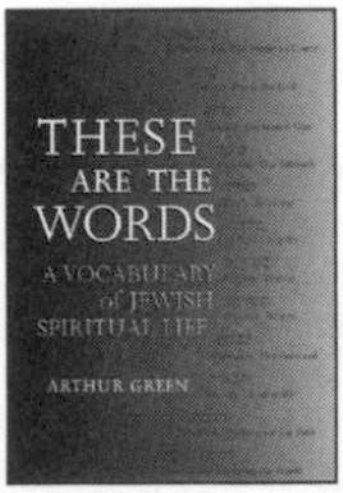

A Heart of Many Rooms: ***Celebrating the Many Voices within Judaism*** AWARD WINNER!
by Dr. David Hartman 6 x 9, 352 pp, Quality PB, ISBN 1-58023-156-X **$19.95**;
HC, ISBN 1-58023-048-2 **$24.95**

A Living Covenant: ***The Innovative Spirit in Traditional Judaism*** AWARD WINNER!
by Dr. David Hartman 6 x 9, 368 pp, Quality PB, ISBN 1-58023-011-3 **$18.95**

Evolving Halakhah: ***A Progressive Approach to Traditional Jewish Law***
by Rabbi Dr. Moshe Zemer 6 x 9, 480 pp, HC, ISBN 1-58023-002-4 **$40.00**

The Death of Death: ***Resurrection and Immortality in Jewish Thought*** AWARD WINNER!
by Dr. Neil Gillman 6 x 9, 336 pp, Quality PB, ISBN 1-58023-081-4 **$18.95**

The Last Trial: ***On the Legends and Lore of the Command to Abraham to Offer Isaac as a Sacrifice*** by Shalom Spiegel 6 x 9, 208 pp, Quality PB, ISBN 1-879045-29-X **$17.95**

Tormented Master: ***The Life and Spiritual Quest of Rabbi Nahman of Bratslav***
by Dr. Arthur Green 6 x 9, 416 pp, Quality PB, ISBN 1-879045-11-7 **$18.95**

The Earth Is the Lord's: ***The Inner World of the Jew in Eastern Europe***
by Abraham Joshua Heschel 5½ x 8, 128 pp, Quality PB, ISBN 1-879045-42-7 **$14.95**

A Passion for Truth: ***Despair and Hope in Hasidism*** by Abraham Joshua Heschel
5½ x 8, 352 pp, Quality PB, ISBN 1-879045-41-9 **$18.95**

Your Word Is Fire: ***The Hasidic Masters on Contemplative Prayer*** Ed. by Dr. Arthur Green and Dr. Barry W. Holtz 6 x 9, 160 pp, Quality PB, ISBN 1-879045-25-7 **$15.95**

Life Cycle/Grief

Against the Dying of the Light
A Parent's Story of Love, Loss and Hope
by *Leonard Fein*

The sudden death of a child. A personal tragedy beyond description. Rage and despair deeper than sorrow. What can come from it? Raw wisdom and defiant hope. In this unusual exploration of heartbreak and healing, Fein chronicles the sudden death of his 30-year-old daughter and reveals what the progression of grief can teach each one of us.
5½ x 8½, 176 pp, HC, ISBN 1-58023-110-1 **$19.95**

Mourning & Mitzvah, 2nd Ed.: *A Guided Journal for Walking the Mourner's Path through Grief to Healing* *with Over 60 Guided Exercises*
by *Anne Brener, L.C.S.W.*

For those who mourn a death, for those who would help them, for those who face a loss of any kind, Brener teaches us the power and strength available to us in the fully experienced mourning process. Revised and expanded. 7½ x 9, 304 pp, Quality PB, ISBN 1-58023-113-6 **$19.95**

Grief in Our Seasons: *A Mourner's Kaddish Companion*
by *Rabbi Kerry M. Olitzky*

A wise and inspiring selection of sacred Jewish writings and a simple, powerful ancient ritual for mourners to read each day, to help hold the memory of their loved ones in their hearts. Offers a comforting, step-by-step daily link to saying Kaddish.
4½ x 6½, 448 pp, Quality PB, ISBN 1-879045-55-9 **$15.95**

Tears of Sorrow, Seeds of Hope
A Jewish Spiritual Companion for Infertility and Pregnancy Loss
by Rabbi Nina Beth Cardin 6 x 9, 192 pp, HC, ISBN 1-58023-017-2 **$19.95**

A Time to Mourn, A Time to Comfort
A Guide to Jewish Bereavement and Comfort
by Dr. Ron Wolfson 7 x 9, 336 pp, Quality PB, ISBN 1-879045-96-6 **$18.95**

When a Grandparent Dies
A Kid's Own Remembering Workbook for Dealing with Shiva and the Year Beyond
by Nechama Liss-Levinson, Ph.D.
8 x 10, 48 pp, HC, Illus., 2-color text, ISBN 1-879045-44-3 **$15.95** **For ages 7–13**

Life Cycle & Holidays

The Jewish Family Fun Book: *Holiday Projects, Everyday Activities, and Travel Ideas with Jewish Themes*

by *Danielle Dardashti* and *Roni Sarig;* Illustrated by *Avi Katz*

With almost 100 easy-to-do activities to re-invigorate age-old Jewish customs and make them fun for the whole family, this complete sourcebook details activities for fun at home and away from home, including meaningful everyday and holiday crafts, recipes, travel guides, enriching entertainment and much, much more. Illustrated.

6 x 9, 288 pp, Quality PB, Illus., ISBN 1-58023-171-3 **$18.95**

The Book of Jewish Sacred Practices
CLAL's Guide to Everyday & Holiday Rituals & Blessings

Ed. by *Rabbi Irwin Kula* & *Vanessa L. Ochs, Ph.D.*

A meditation, blessing, profound Jewish teaching, and ritual for more than one hundred everyday events and holidays. 6 x 9, 368 pp, Quality PB, ISBN 1-58023-152-7 **$18.95**

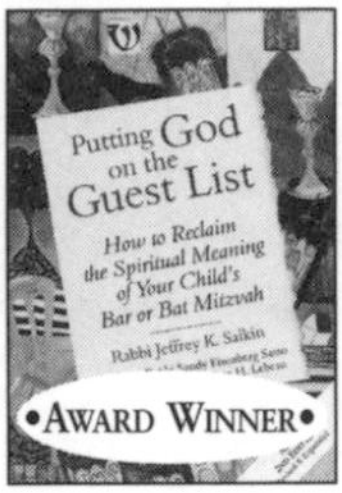

Celebrating Your New Jewish Daughter: *Creating Jewish Ways to Welcome Baby Girls into the Covenant—New and Traditional Ceremonies*
by Debra Nussbaum Cohen; Foreword by Rabbi Sandy Eisenberg Sasso
6 x 9, 272 pp, Quality PB, ISBN 1-58023-090-3 **$18.95**

The New Jewish Baby Book AWARD WINNER!
Names, Ceremonies & Customs—A Guide for Today's Families
by Anita Diamant 6 x 9, 336 pp, Quality PB, ISBN 1-879045-28-1 **$18.95**

Parenting As a Spiritual Journey
Deepening Ordinary & Extraordinary Events into Sacred Occasions
by Rabbi Nancy Fuchs-Kreimer 6 x 9, 224 pp, Quality PB, ISBN 1-58023-016-4 **$16.95**

Putting God on the Guest List, 2nd Ed. AWARD WINNER!
How to Reclaim the Spiritual Meaning of Your Child's Bar or Bat Mitzvah
by Rabbi Jeffrey K. Salkin 6 x 9, 224 pp, Quality PB, ISBN 1-879045-59-1 **$16.95**

The Bar/Bat Mitzvah Memory Book: *An Album for Treasuring the Spiritual Celebration* by Rabbi Jeffrey K. Salkin and Nina Salkin
8 x 10, 48 pp, Deluxe HC, 2-color text, ribbon marker, ISBN 1-58023-111-X **$19.95**

For Kids—Putting God on Your Guest List
How to Claim the Spiritual Meaning of Your Bar or Bat Mitzvah
by Rabbi Jeffrey K. Salkin 6 x 9, 144 pp, Quality PB, ISBN 1-58023-015-6 **$14.95**

Bar/Bat Mitzvah Basics, 2nd Ed.: *A Practical Family Guide to Coming of Age Together*
Ed. by Cantor Helen Leneman 6 x 9, 240 pp, Quality PB, ISBN 1-58023-151-9 **$18.95**

Hanukkah, 2nd Ed.: *The Family Guide to Spiritual Celebration*—The Art of Jewish Living
by Dr. Ron Wolfson 7 x 9, 240 pp, Quality PB, Illus., ISBN 1-58023-122-5 **$18.95**

Shabbat, 2nd Ed.: *Preparing for and Celebrating the Sabbath*—The Art of Jewish Living
by Dr. Ron Wolfson 7 x 9, 320 pp, Quality PB, Illus., ISBN 1-58023-164-0 **$19.95**

The Passover Seder—The Art of Jewish Living
by Dr. Ron Wolfson 7 x 9, 352 pp, Quality PB, Illus., ISBN 1-879045-93-1 **$16.95**

Healing/Wellness/Recovery

Jewish Paths toward Healing and Wholeness
A Personal Guide to Dealing with Suffering

by *Rabbi Kerry M. Olitzky;* Foreword by *Debbie Friedman*

Why me? Why do we suffer? How can we heal? Grounded in personal experience with illness and Jewish spiritual traditions, this book provides healing rituals, psalms and prayers that help readers initiate a dialogue with God, to guide them along the complicated path of healing and wholeness. 6 x 9, 192 pp, Quality PB, ISBN 1-58023-068-7 **$15.95**

Healing of Soul, Healing of Body
Spiritual Leaders Unfold the Strength & Solace in Psalms

Ed. by *Rabbi Simkha Y. Weintraub, CSW,* for The National Center for Jewish Healing

For those who are facing illness and those who care for them. Inspiring commentaries on ten psalms for healing by eminent spiritual leaders reflecting all Jewish movements make the power of the psalms accessible to all.
6 x 9, 128 pp, Quality PB, Illus., 2-color text, ISBN 1-879045-31-1 **$14.95**

Jewish Pastoral Care
A Practical Handbook from Traditional and Contemporary Sources

Ed. by *Rabbi Dayle A. Friedman*

Gives today's Jewish pastoral counselors practical guidelines based in the Jewish tradition.
6 x 9, 464 pp, HC, ISBN 1-58023-078-4 **$35.00**

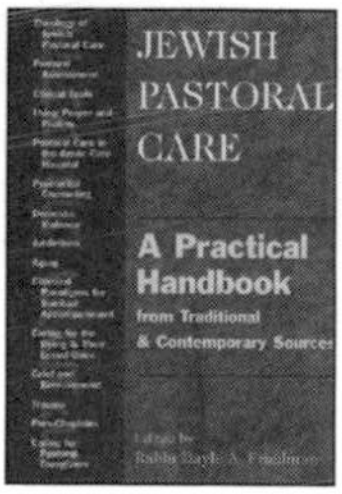

Twelve Jewish Steps to Recovery: ***A Personal Guide to Turning from Alcoholism & Other Addictions . . . Drugs, Food, Gambling, Sex . . .*** by Rabbi Kerry M. Olitzky & Stuart A. Copans, M.D. Preface by Abraham J. Twerski, M.D.; "Getting Help" by JACS Foundation 6 x 9, 144 pp, Quality PB, ISBN 1-879045-09-5 **$13.95**

One Hundred Blessings Every Day: ***Daily Twelve Step Recovery Affirmations, Exercises for Personal Growth & Renewal Reflecting Seasons of the Jewish Year*** by Rabbi Kerry M. Olitzky 4½ x 6½, 432 pp, Quality PB, ISBN 1-879045-30-3 **$14.95**

Recovery from Codependence: ***A Jewish Twelve Steps Guide to Healing Your Soul*** by Rabbi Kerry M. Olitzky 6 x 9, 160 pp, Quality PB, ISBN 1-879045-32-X **$13.95**

Renewed Each Day: ***Daily Twelve Step Recovery Meditations Based on the Bible*** by Rabbi Kerry M. Olitzky & Aaron Z. *Vol. I: Genesis & Exodus*; *Vol. II: Leviticus, Numbers and Deuteronomy*
Vol. I: 6 x 9, 224 pp, Quality PB, ISBN 1-879045-12-5 **$14.95**
Vol. II: 6 x 9, 280 pp, Quality PB, ISBN 1-879045-13-3 **$14.95**

Spirituality—The Kushner Series

Books by Lawrence Kushner

The Way Into Jewish Mystical Tradition

Explains the principles of Jewish mystical thinking, their religious and spiritual significance, and how they relate to our lives. A book that allows us to experience and understand the Jewish mystical approach to our place in the world.
6 x 9, 224 pp, HC, ISBN 1-58023-029-6 **$21.95**

Jewish Spirituality: *A Brief Introduction for Christians*

Addresses Christian's questions, revealing the essence of Judaism in a way that people whose own tradition traces its roots to Judaism can understand and appreciate.
5½ x 8½, 112 pp, Quality PB, ISBN 1-58023-150-0 **$12.95**

Eyes Remade for Wonder: *The Way of Jewish Mysticism and Sacred Living*

A Lawrence Kushner Reader Intro. by *Thomas Moore*

Whether you are new to Kushner or a devoted fan, you'll find inspiration here. With samplings from each of Kushner's works, and a generous amount of new material, this book is to be read and reread, each time discovering deeper layers of meaning in our lives.
6 x 9, 240 pp, Quality PB, ISBN 1-58023-042-3 **$16.95**; HC, ISBN 1-58023-014-8 **$23.95**

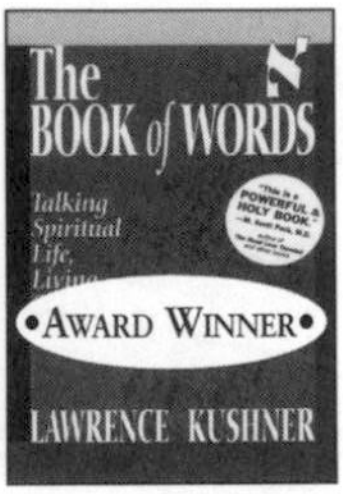

Invisible Lines of Connection: *Sacred Stories of the Ordinary* **AWARD WINNER!**
5½ x 8½, 160 pp, Quality PB, ISBN 1-879045-98-2 **$15.95**

Honey from the Rock: *An Introduction to Jewish Mysticism* **SPECIAL ANNIVERSARY EDITION**
6 x 9, 176 pp, Quality PB, ISBN 1-58023-073-3 **$15.95**

The Book of Letters: *A Mystical Hebrew Alphabet* **AWARD WINNER!**
Popular HC Edition, 6 x 9, 80 pp, 2-color text, ISBN 1-879045-00-1 **$24.95**; *Deluxe Gift Edition,* 9 x 12, 80 pp, HC, 4-color text, ornamentation, slipcase, ISBN 1-879045-01-X **$79.95**; *Collector's Limited Edition,* 9 x 12, 80 pp, HC, gold-embossed pages, hand-assembled slipcase. With silkscreened print. Limited to 500 signed and numbered copies, ISBN 1-879045-04-4 **$349.00**

The Book of Words: *Talking Spiritual Life, Living Spiritual Talk* **AWARD WINNER!**
6 x 9, 160 pp, Quality PB, 2-color text, ISBN 1-58023-020-2 **$16.95**; HC, ISBN 1-879045-35-4 **$21.95**

God Was in This Place & I, i Did Not Know: *Finding Self, Spirituality and Ultimate Meaning*
6 x 9, 192 pp, Quality PB, ISBN 1-879045-33-8 **$16.95**

The River of Light: *Jewish Mystical Awareness* **SPECIAL ANNIVERSARY EDITION**
6 x 9, 192 pp, Quality PB, ISBN 1-58023-096-2 **$16.95**

Because Nothing Looks Like God
by Lawrence and Karen Kushner; Full-color illus. by Dawn W. Majewski
11 x 8½, 32 pp, HC, Full-color illus., ISBN 1-58023-092-X **$16.95** **For ages 4 & up**

Children's Spirituality

ENDORSED BY CATHOLIC, PROTESTANT, AND JEWISH RELIGIOUS LEADERS

Because Nothing Looks Like God

by *Lawrence and Karen Kushner*
Full-color illus. by *Dawn W. Majewski*

For ages 4 & up

MULTICULTURAL, NONDENOMINATIONAL, NONSECTARIAN

What is God like? The first collaborative work by husband-and-wife team Lawrence and Karen Kushner introduces children to the possibilities of spiritual life. Real-life examples of happiness and sadness—from goodnight stories, to the hope and fear felt the first time at bat, to the closing moments of life—invite us to explore, together with our children, the questions we all have about God, no matter what our age.

11 x 8½, 32 pp, HC, Full-color illus., ISBN 1-58023-092-X **$16.95**

Where Is God?
What Does God Look Like?
How Does God Make Things Happen? (Board Books)

For ages 0–4

by *Lawrence and Karen Kushner;* Full-color illus. by *Dawn W. Majewski*

Gently invites children to become aware of God's presence all around them. Three board books abridged from *Because Nothing Looks Like God* by Lawrence and Karen Kushner.

Each 5 x 5, 24 pp, Board, Full-color illus. **$7.95** SKYLIGHT PATHS Books

Sharing Blessings
Children's Stories for Exploring the Spirit of the Jewish Holidays

For ages 6 & up

by *Rahel Musleah* and *Rabbi Michael Klayman;* Full-color illus.

What is the spiritual message of each of the Jewish holidays? How do we teach it to our children? Through stories about one family's life, *Sharing Blessings* explores ways to get into the *spirit* of thirteen different holidays.

8½ x 11, 64 pp, HC, Full-color illus., ISBN 1-879045-71-0 **$18.95**

The Book of Miracles AWARD WINNER!
A Young Person's Guide to Jewish Spiritual Awareness

For ages 9 & up

by *Lawrence Kushner*

Introduces kids to a way of everyday spiritual thinking to last a lifetime. Kushner, whose award-winning books have brought spirituality to life for countless adults, now shows young people how to use Judaism as a foundation on which to build their lives.

6 x 9, 96 pp, HC, 2-color illus., ISBN 1-879045-78-8 **$16.95**

Children's Spirituality

ENDORSED BY CATHOLIC, PROTESTANT, AND JEWISH RELIGIOUS LEADERS
MULTICULTURAL, NONDENOMINATIONAL, NONSECTARIAN

In Our Image
God's First Creatures AWARD WINNER!

For ages 4 & up

by *Nancy Sohn Swartz*
Full-color illus. by *Melanie Hall*

A playful new twist on the Creation story—from the perspective of the animals. Celebrates the interconnectedness of nature and the harmony of all living things. "The vibrantly colored illustrations nearly leap off the page in this delightful interpretation." —*School Library Journal*
9 x 12, 32 pp, HC, Full-color illus., ISBN 1-879045-99-0 **$16.95**

God's Paintbrush AWARD WINNER!

For ages 4 & up

by *Sandy Eisenberg Sasso;* Full-color illus. by *Annette Compton*

Invites children of all faiths and backgrounds to encounter God openly in their own lives. Wonderfully interactive; provides questions adult and child can explore together at the end of each episode. 11 x 8½, 32 pp, HC, Full-color illus., ISBN 1-879045-22-2 **$16.95**

Also available: ***A Teacher's Guide:*** **A Guide for Jewish & Christian Educators and Parents**
8½ x 11, 32 pp, PB, ISBN 1-879045-57-5 **$8.95**

God's Paintbrush Celebration Kit 9½ x 12, HC, Includes 5 sessions/40 full-color Activity Sheets and Teacher Folder with complete instructions, ISBN 1-58023-050-4 **$21.95**

In God's Name AWARD WINNER!

For ages 4 & up

by *Sandy Eisenberg Sasso;* Full-color illus. by *Phoebe Stone*

Like an ancient myth in its poetic text and vibrant illustrations, this award-winning modern fable about the search for God's name celebrates the diversity and, at the same time, the unity of all people. 9 x 12, 32 pp, HC, Full-color illus., ISBN 1-879045-26-5 **$16.95**

What Is God's Name? (A Board Book)

For ages 0–4

An abridged board book version of award-winning *In God's Name.*
5 x 5, 24 pp, Board, Full-color illus., ISBN 1-893361-10-1 **$7.95** A SKYLIGHT PATHS Book

The 11th Commandment: *Wisdom from Our Children*

For all ages

by *The Children of America* **AWARD WINNER!**

"If there were an Eleventh Commandment, what would it be?" Children of many religious denominations across America answer this question—in their own drawings and words. "A rare book of spiritual celebration for all people, of all ages, for all time."—*Bookviews*
8 x 10, 48 pp, HC, Full-color illus., ISBN 1-879045-46-X **$16.95**

Children's Spirituality

ENDORSED BY CATHOLIC, PROTESTANT, AND JEWISH RELIGIOUS LEADERS
MULTICULTURAL, NONDENOMINATIONAL, NONSECTARIAN

Cain & Abel AWARD WINNER!
Finding the Fruits of Peace

For ages 5 & up

by *Sandy Eisenberg Sasso*
Full-color illus. by *Joani Keller Rothenberg*

A sensitive recasting of the ancient tale shows we have the power to deal with anger in positive ways. Provides questions for kids and adults to explore together. "Editor's Choice"—American Library Association's *Booklist*

9 x 12, 32 pp, HC, Full-color illus., ISBN 1-58023-123-3 **$16.95**

For Heaven's Sake AWARD WINNER!

For ages 4 & up

by *Sandy Eisenberg Sasso;* Full-color illus. by *Kathryn Kunz Finney*

Everyone talked about heaven, but no one would say what heaven was or how to find it. So Isaiah decides to find out. 9 x 12, 32 pp, HC, Full-color illus., ISBN 1-58023-054-7 **$16.95**

God Said Amen AWARD WINNER!

For ages 4 & up

by *Sandy Eisenberg Sasso;* Full-color illus. by *Avi Katz*

Inspiring tale of two kingdoms: one overflowing with water but without oil to light its lamps; the other blessed with oil but no water to grow its gardens. The kingdoms' rulers ask God for help but are too stubborn to ask each other. Shows that we need only reach out to each other to find God's answer to our prayers. 9 x 12, 32 pp, HC, Full-color illus., ISBN 1-58023-080-6 **$16.95**

God in Between AWARD WINNER!

For ages 4 & up

by *Sandy Eisenberg Sasso;* Full-color illus. by *Sally Sweetland*

If you wanted to find God, where would you look? This magical, mythical tale teaches that God can be found where we are: within all of us and the relationships between us.
9 x 12, 32 pp, HC, Full-color illus., ISBN 1-879045-86-9 **$16.95**

A Prayer for the Earth: *The Story of Naamah, Noah's Wife*

For ages 4 & up

by *Sandy Eisenberg Sasso;* Full-color illus. by *Bethanne Andersen* AWARD WINNER!

Opens religious imaginations to new ideas about the story of the Flood. When God tells Noah to bring the animals onto the ark, God also calls on Naamah, Noah's wife, to save each plant on Earth. 9 x 12, 32 pp, HC, Full-color illus., ISBN 1-879045-60-5 **$16.95**

But God Remembered AWARD WINNER!
Stories of Women from Creation to the Promised Land

For ages 8 & up

by *Sandy Eisenberg Sasso;* Full-color illus. by *Bethanne Andersen*

Vibrantly brings to life four stories of courageous and strong women from ancient tradition; all teach important values through their actions and faith.
9 x 12, 32 pp, HC, Full-color illus., ISBN 1-879045-43-5 **$16.95**

Spirituality & More

The Jewish Lights Spirituality Handbook
A Guide to Understanding, Exploring & Living a Spiritual Life

Ed. by *Stuart M. Matlins, Editor-in-Chief, Jewish Lights Publishing*

Rich, creative material from over fifty spiritual leaders on every aspect of Jewish spirituality today: prayer, meditation, mysticism, study, rituals, special days, the everyday, and more.
6 x 9, 456 pp, Quality PB, ISBN 1-58023-093-8 **$18.95**; HC, ISBN 1-58023-100-4 **$24.95**

The Story of the Jews: *A 4,000-Year Adventure—A Graphic History Book*

Written and illustrated by *Stan Mack*

Through witty cartoons and accurate narrative, illustrates the major characters and events that have shaped the Jewish people and culture. For all ages.
6 x 9, 304 pp, Quality PB, Illus., ISBN 1-58023-155-1 **$16.95**

The Jewish Prophet: *Visionary Words from Moses and Miriam to Henrietta Szold and A. J. Heschel*

by *Rabbi Dr. Michael J. Shire*

This beautifully illustrated collection of Jewish prophecy features the lives and teachings of thirty men and women, from biblical times to modern day. Provides an inspiring and informative description of the role each played in their own time, and an explanation of why we should know about them in our time. Illustrated with illuminations from medieval Hebrew manuscripts.
6½ x 8½, 128 pp, HC, 123 full-color illus., ISBN 1-58023-168-3 **$25.00**

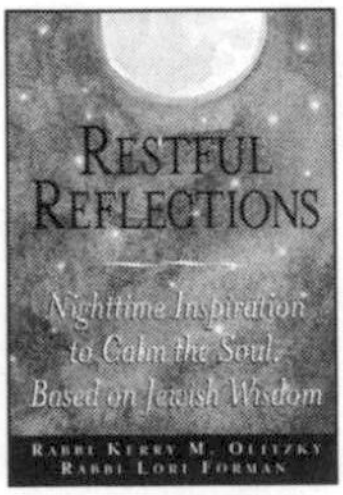

The Enneagram and Kabbalah: *Reading Your Soul*
by Rabbi Howard A. Addison 6 x 9, 176 pp, Quality PB, ISBN 1-58023-001-6 **$15.95**

Cast in God's Image: *Discover Your Personality Type Using the Enneagram and Kabbalah*
by Rabbi Howard A. Addison 7 x 9, 176 pp, Quality PB, ISBN 1-58023-124-1 **$16.95**

Mystery Midrash: *An Anthology of Jewish Mystery & Detective Fiction* AWARD WINNER!
Ed. by Lawrence W. Raphael 6 x 9, 304 pp, Quality PB, ISBN 1-58023-055-5 **$16.95**

Criminal Kabbalah: *An Intriguing Anthology of Jewish Mystery & Detective Fiction*
Ed. by Lawrence W. Raphael; Foreword by Laurie R. King
6 x 9, 256 pp, Quality PB, ISBN 1-58023-109-8 **$16.95**

Sacred Intentions: *Daily Inspiration to Strengthen the Spirit, Based on Jewish Wisdom*
by Rabbi Kerry M. Olitzky & Rabbi Lori Forman
4½ x 6½, 448 pp, Quality PB, ISBN 1-58023-061-X **$15.95**

Restful Reflections: *Nighttime Inspiration to Calm the Soul, Based on Jewish Wisdom*
by Rabbi Kerry M. Olitzky & Rabbi Lori Forman
4½ x 6½, 448 pp, Quality PB, ISBN 1-58023-091-1 **$15.95**

Embracing the Covenant: *Converts to Judaism Talk About Why & How* Ed. by Rabbi Allan Berkowitz & Patti Moskovitz 6 x 9, 192 pp, Quality PB, ISBN 1-879045-50-8 **$16.95**

Wandering Stars: *An Anthology of Jewish Fantasy & Science Fiction* Ed. by Jack Dann; Intro. by Isaac Asimov 6 x 9, 272 pp, Quality PB, ISBN 1-58023-005-9 **$16.95**

Israel—A Spiritual Travel Guide: *A Companion for the Modern Jewish Pilgrim* AWARD WINNER!
by Rabbi Lawrence A. Hoffman 4¾ x 10, 256 pp, Quality PB, ISBN 1-879045-56-7 **$18.95**

Women's Spirituality

The Women's Torah Commentary: ***New Insights from Women Rabbis on the 54 Weekly Torah Portions*** Ed. by *Rabbi Elyse Goldstein*

For the first time, women rabbis provide a commentary on the entire Five Books of Moses. More than twenty-five years after the first woman was ordained a rabbi in America, these inspiring teachers bring their rich perspectives to bear on the biblical text. In a week-by-week format; a perfect gift for others, or for yourself. 6 x 9, 496 pp, HC, ISBN 1-58023-076-8 **$34.95**

Moonbeams: ***A Hadassah Rosh Hodesh Guide***

Ed. by *Carol Diament, Ph.D.*

This hands-on "idea book" focuses on *Rosh Hodesh,* the festival of the new moon, as a source of spiritual growth for Jewish women. A complete sourcebook that will initiate or rejuvenate women's study groups, it is also perfect for women preparing for *bat mitzvah*, or for anyone interested in learning more about *Rosh Hodesh* observance and what it has to offer. 8½ x 11, 240 pp, Quality PB, ISBN 1-58023-099-7 **$20.00**

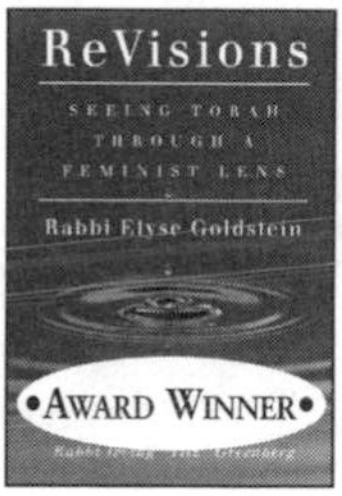

Lifecycles In Two Volumes **AWARD WINNERS!**
V. 1: ***Jewish Women on Life Passages & Personal Milestones***
Ed. and with Intros. by Rabbi Debra Orenstein
V. 2: ***Jewish Women on Biblical Themes in Contemporary Life***
Ed. and with Intros. by Rabbi Debra Orenstein and Rabbi Jane Rachel Litman
V. 1: 6 x 9, 480 pp, Quality PB, ISBN 1-58023-018-0 **$19.95**
V. 2: 6 x 9, 464 pp, Quality PB, ISBN 1-58023-019-9 **$19.95**

ReVisions: ***Seeing Torah through a Feminist Lens*** **AWARD WINNER!**
by Rabbi Elyse Goldstein 5½ x 8½, 224 pp, Quality PB, ISBN 1-58023-117-9 **$16.95**; 208 pp, HC, ISBN 1-58023-047-4 **$19.95**

The Year Mom Got Religion: ***One Woman's Midlife Journey into Judaism***
by Lee Meyerhoff Hendler 6 x 9, 208 pp, Quality PB, ISBN 1-58023-070-9 **$15.95**

Ecology

Torah of the Earth: ***Exploring 4,000 Years of Ecology in Jewish Thought***
In 2 Volumes Ed. by *Rabbi Arthur Waskow*

An invaluable key to understanding the intersection of ecology and Judaism. Leading scholars provide a guided tour of Jewish ecological thought.
Vol. 1: *Biblical Israel & Rabbinic Judaism,* 6 x 9, 272 pp, Quality PB, ISBN 1-58023-086-5 **$19.95**
Vol. 2: *Zionism & Eco-Judaism,* 6 x 9, 336 pp, Quality PB, ISBN 1-58023-087-3 **$19.95**

Ecology & the Jewish Spirit: ***Where Nature & the Sacred Meet*** Ed. and with Intros. by Ellen Bernstein 6 x 9, 288 pp, Quality PB, ISBN 1-58023-082-2 **$16.95**

The Jewish Gardening Cookbook: ***Growing Plants & Cooking for Holidays & Festivals***
by Michael Brown 6 x 9, 224 pp, Illus., Quality PB, ISBN 1-58023-116-0 **$16.95**; HC, ISBN 1-58023-004-0 **$21.95**